Scummy Mummies

Ellie Gibson
& Helen Thorn

A CELEBRATION OF PARENTING
FAILURES, HILARIOUS CONFESSIONS,
FISH FINGERS AND WINE

quadrille

FOR MATILDA, HUGO,
CHARLIE AND JOE,
WHO ARE THE SOURCE OF
SUCH LOVE AND JOY
AND SO MUCH MATERIAL.

Publishing director: Sarah Lavelle
Creative director: Helen Lewis
Commissioning editor: Céline Hughes
Designer: Emily Lapworth
Production: Steve McCabe,
 Vincent Smith

Front cover photograph
© 2017 Giada Garofalo
Inside back cover photograph
© 2017 Joseph Fox
Front cover hand lettering

First published in
Quadrille Publishi
Pentagon House,
52–54 Southwark S
London SE1 1UN

Quadrille Publishi
imprint of Hardie
www.hardiegrant.c
www.quadrille.co.u

Text © Ellie Gibso
and Helen Thorn
Design and layout
© 2017 Quadrille Publishing

CONTENTS

DEAR FELLOW SCUMMY MUMMY

Dear fellow Scummy Mummy,

We know your secrets. We know you gave the kids fish fingers four times in a row last week. We know you drink wine out of a mug at teatime. We know that once your son did a sick in Sainsbury's, and you ran away.

We know you forgot your daughter's name when another mum asked, even though she's an only child. We know you used one of your son's toys to fish a poo out of the bath, giving a whole new meaning to the term 'dump truck'.

We know you sneaked wine into a classical music concert by hiding it in your child's beaker. Or as you prefer to call it, the Tommee Tipsee.

We know about that rainy Thursday when you let your kids watch *Madagascar* twice in a row while you sat in the kitchen and did Google image searches for Benedict Cumberbatch.

We know you picked up that raisin you found on the stairs and popped it in your mouth. Only to discover it wasn't a raisin.

We know that one Sunday afternoon, you let the kids cut each other's hair while you finished the wine.

We know you pretend not to notice when your child eats chicken nuggets the cat has just licked.

We know that right now, there's a dirty nappy in your handbag.

We know about all these things because you shared them with us. Some of you told us after listening to our podcast. Some of you confessed at our comedy show. Some of them are things we've done ourselves. Because no matter how hard we try, at some point, all parents end up doing something scummy.

Still wondering what a Scummy Mummy is? Basically, it's the opposite of a Yummy Mummy.

Yummy Mummy	Scummy Mummy
Feeds her children lovely organic quinoa and kale sandwiches every day.	Feeds her kids fish fingers every day. Sometimes not even cooked. (Mmm, Captain Birdseye sashimi.)
Teaches her kids to play the violin.	Teaches her kids to play *Angry Birds*.
Takes her children on long woodland walks to collect leaves for an autumnal collage.	Takes her children to Lidl to see how many different kinds of foreign crisps they can spot. Crusti Croc safari!
Has children who can sight-read music and spend hours practising for their ballet recital.	Has children who know all the words and dance moves to *Gangnam Style*. Hey, sexy lady!
Prepares a fresh papaya and wheatgrass smoothie every morning.	Counts Fruit Shoot as one of her five-a-day.
Has children who are fluent in French.	Has children who are fluent in CBeebies, having watched so much TV they think Mr Tumble is their dad.
Ensures her children are able to do complex equations and use an abacus by the age of six.	Teaches her kids how to write BOOBIES on a calculator.

The fact is, not one of us is perfect – not even Kirstie Allsopp. As Scummy Mummies, if there's one phrase that comes to mind when we think about our parenting style, it's this: 'Let it go.' And not because we've been forced to sit through that bloody DVD so many times that one of us once shouted "OLAF!" at the point of climax.

Of course, it's important to make sure your kids are loved, fed and relatively clean. But there are some things we don't think it's worth worrying about. For instance:

A Clean House for Play Dates
"Oh no! The girls are coming over for coffee – I'd better get up at 5AM to bleach the toilet and hand-make some spelt truffles!" Fuck this shit.

Anyone who gives a toss if there's Lego all over the floor can go in the bin. The good people won't care, and the best people will say, "Oh, this makes me feel better about my own shithole." These are the keepers.

Ironing
Unless there is an actual emergency – like a job interview, or your mother-in-law is coming over from Australia – put the ironing board down, people. The kids won't care if their jeans are a bit crumpled. If you have a baby, all your clothes will be covered in snot and porridge by 9AM anyway.

Perfect Homemade Cakes
Look, we feel your pain. One of us was recently up until 2AM creating a fondant unicorn oasis that Paul Hollywood would have described as "a bit elaborate". Twelve hours later, we watched a group of six-year-olds rip it to shreds in under a minute.

All kids care about is the quantity of Smarties and the volume of icing. In fact, why not just stick a few candles in a bag of sugar?

Creative Meals
There's no need to spend hours creating Picassos out of peas and potatoes. If your kids will only eat a few things, give yourself a break. Humans can survive on pasta and sweetcorn. And don't

compare yourself to the woman at the Giraffe café in Blackheath whose children were asking for the bulgur wheat salad. She wasn't real – it was just an apparition, because you were so tired.

Being Everyone's BEST FRIEND

When your kid starts nursery or school, the number of new potential friends and social gatherings can be overwhelming. It's good to be polite and friendly, but you don't have to be everyone's best mate.

Remember, your time is precious. What would you rather do, have a pint with that old drinking buddy you haven't seen since your twenties, or sit in a Caffè Nero with someone you barely know talking about house prices?

Feeling Like You and Your Kids Are Not Normal

This is one of the great anxieties of parenting. Is what your kids are into normal? What about the food they eat? Or the fact they like singing Kanye West songs at the top of their voices on the number 75 bus?

Worrying about these things can leave you feeling isolated and crappy. But here's the thing: there IS no normal. Just like people, all families are different, and they're all a bit weird in their own way.

And because of this, there is no such thing as a one-size-fits-all parenting style. The trick is to find out what works for you and your kids, and try not to worry too much about what everyone else thinks. The c***s never bothered you anyway.

Just ask yourself: is your child happy? Does he know he is loved? Does she have clean knickers on at least 300 days of the year? Then you are doing a good job.

We might have different ways of parenting, but putting each other down is a waste of our time and energy. Two things will always unite us: we love our children, and we are all scummy mummies. So let's be united in our failures. Let's talk to each other, and share our scummy stories, and be honest about our imperfections. Most of all, let's have a good laugh.

FROM SHAGGING TO SHOUTING: IS THERE SEX LIFE AFTER KIDS?

Parenthood changes your relationship with your partner in so many ways. But don't focus on the loss of your carefree romantic lifestyle – think about what you're gaining! Who needs sex and laughter when you've got fighting and fish fingers?

Sure, before kids, you were free to stay out till dawn, have sex whenever you felt like it and eat an entire meal without shouting at anyone to stop putting peas up their nose. But now you'll find new ways to express your feelings for each other, like angry texts, whispered swearing and poking each other in the middle of the night until SOMEONE GETS THE BABY.

Then there are the benefits of things like breastfeeding, which can give you big, gorgeous boobs just like Pamela Anderson – if she spent all day having to replace soggy breast pads in her red swimsuit. Nothing creates a romantic atmosphere like fixing your husband with a death stare whenever he comes within three metres of your milk jugs, while muttering, "Don't you even THINK about touching my tits." Sexy times!

Let's be honest: getting busy in the bedroom is less of a priority if you barely have the energy to take off your own

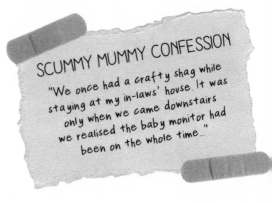

SCUMMY MUMMY CONFESSION

"We once had a crafty shag while staying at my in-laws' house. It was only when we came downstairs we realised the baby monitor had been on the whole time..."

socks. When you've been awake all night with a baby, it's hard to remember what attracted you to your partner in the first place, or that you don't hate them.

But don't worry if you find yourselves arguing all the time. Just think about all that make-up sex! Although after you've had kids, it's usually more about the wake-up sex – which is where you have to wake each other up in the middle of it.

The important thing is to make time for each other. A great tip is to schedule sex in your diary (because nothing is as erotic as appointments). Just slot it in between teatime, bedtime, emptying the dishwasher, hanging the laundry out, rowing, ringing the plumber, filling out 17 school forms, rowing, defleaing the dog, finding the other shoe, unclogging the drain, renewing the car insurance, putting the bins out, and rowing. Basically, plan to have sex between 1.42AM and 1.45AM.

Here's the bottom line: don't worry about how much sex you're having, how often everyone else is at it, or how your sex life has changed. Who cares if you've swapped S&M for M&S, or anal play for an annual bunk-up? If you're doing it at all, you're doing great.

BEFORE AND AFTER: SEX

Sex changes after you've had kids. Suddenly 'Netflix and chill' literally means watching eight minutes of *Making a Murderer* before passing out in a pool of your own drool. And your reasons for having it off change, as this handy table illustrates.

Before kids	After kids
For fun	To conceive another child
Because you like each other	It's someone's birthday, so you're pretending to like each other
To feel more connected on an emotional, physical and spiritual level	You had an erotic dream about Jeff Goldblum, and feel confident you can maintain the illusion if you close your eyes
Because it's been over a week	Because it's been over a month
To try out an exciting new position you saw in *Cosmo*	Because it's been over six months
Your housemates are out	The kids got a Pixar box set for Christmas
There's nothing on TV	There's nothing on TV
You're pissed	You're pissed

HOW TO HAVE A GREAT DATE NIGHT

If you feel the spark has gone out of your relationship, why not try going out on some dates? Perhaps with each other. It'll be just like old times! Except totally different. Here are our top tips for having an awesome date night, post-kids.

Leave the House Relaxed
Try to make sure your kids are tired and in peak tantrum mode when you head out for the night. Nothing sets the tone for the evening better than a four-year-old screaming "NOOOO! PLEEEEEEEEEEASE MUMMY DON'T GOOOOOOOOOOOO!" Everyone will feel relaxed and ready to party.

Wear Something Special
Show you've made an effort by wearing an item of clothing with only one bodily fluid on it. Or ring the changes by picking something you haven't worn for a few years that no longer fits. Don't worry if you haven't had a shower for a few days – just freshen up with an entire can of Batiste and a squirt from a bottle of CK One that went off back in 2009.

Be Hungry for It
It's best to go on a date when you are starving. Your blood sugar will be low, and you will resort to raw animal instincts, like growling. This is great for creating an intimate atmosphere.

Play Hard to Get
There's nothing sexy about appearing too interested. Keep your phone to hand at all times and don't be afraid to send a few work emails, check Facebook and reply to that text from your friend about where to buy nit combs. Better still, take a selfie and post it on Instagram to tell everyone you're having a great night out while totally ignoring your partner.

Find the Perfect Spot
Getting through challenges brings couples closer, so pick a restaurant that has inadequate parking, terrible reviews on TripAdvisor and is closed. Make sure you wear ill-fitting heels in

preparation for the 20-minute trudge round local streets before you give up and go to a Wetherspoon's pub.

Put Sex on the Menu
It's a special night, so go heavy on the red wine, but don't forget to line your stomach with tons of carbs and starch. This will start the bloating process and enhance the sensation of exhaustion you were experiencing before you even left the house. Erotic!

Keep the Conversation Flowing
This is an opportunity for you to chat about things you never get the chance to discuss at home, like that unpaid Council Tax bill, or what you really think of each other's family. Honesty can be a real aphrodisiac, so add a bit of spice to the conversation by starting sentences with the phrase: "Do you know what really fucks me off?"

Do It Fast and Hard
Add an exciting frisson of urgency to your date by employing an extortionately expensive babysitter who has to be home by 10PM. There's nothing like scoffing your food so fast you get indigestion and making a mad dash for the last train to make you feel aroused.

Slip Between the Sheets
After all that build-up, it's great to get home, get into bed and get down to the thing you've been looking forward to all evening: SLEEP.

ACTUAL TOP TIP
Sarah Lorentzen, fanny physio to the stars
"Sex after childbirth? Is there any? YES! But wait until your undercarriage is ready. At three months post-birth, only 50% of women have even considered it, so there's no hurry. When you're ready, close your eyes, open your legs, think of England and give it a (gentle) go. Sure, it probably won't be a swinging-from-the-chandeliers-multiple-orgasm kind of shag, but at least you made the effort. And if pain persists, see your local fanny physio (women's-health physiotherapist, if you want the official term.)"

SEX POSITIONS FOR PARENTS

Forget the Wheelbarrow, the Reverse Cowgirl and the Upside-down Lotus Blossom. No one with kids has the energy for all that. Here are some more feasible sex positions to try.

The Multitasker
Classic doggy style, but on the kitchen floor. Then you can save time by having sex while picking up old Cheerios.

Silent Night
Ramp up the erotic tension by constantly telling your partner to be quiet in case he wakes the baby.

Eyes Wide Shut
Have sex blindfolded. It's not an S&M thing; it's so you don't have to see all the piles of dirty washing or kids' toys. Suddenly finding yourself staring into Iggle Piggle's cold dead eyes can really ruin the moment for you.

Rhythm Method
Worried your partner is about to climax too soon? Make them last longer by singing a rousing verse of *Wind the Bobbin Up.*

Sexy Buffet
Treat your partner to an erotic feast by covering your naked body with sushi. If you don't have any sushi to hand, try covering your nipples with Mini Babybels and filling your belly button with hummus. It's up to you where you put the breadsticks...

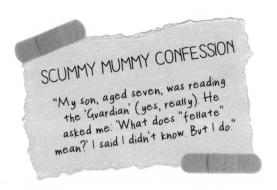

SCUMMY MUMMY CONFESSION

"My son, aged seven, was reading the 'Guardian' (yes, really). He asked me: 'What does "fellate" mean?' I said I didn't know. But I do."

TRUE STORIES: ELLIE

Some days, being a parent feels like being Bear Grylls. My top priorities are shelter (ringing that bloody plumber about the leak under the sink), fire (turning the central heating up without my husband noticing), food (oh God, have we run out of frozen pizza?), and water (wine).

Sex does not feature on that list. But it's not on Bear's list, either. You don't see him taking a break from weaving bulrushes and drinking his own piss to knock one out behind a nettle bush, do you?

Obviously, sex is great and fun and key to maintaining a healthy relationship and all that. But now we've got small children, I feel like what's really keeping my husband and me together is a mutual love of junk food.

This always becomes apparent around the time of our anniversary. (The anniversary of our wedding, not of the last time we had sex. Although some years it has been both.)

Last year, my husband suggested a night in.

"We'll watch a film, get a curry and then, you know, a bit of the other..."

"What," I said, "get a Chinese as well?"

Once that misunderstanding had been cleared up, I explained I didn't fancy a curry, because I always end up bloated and farty – and not super-sexy.

"I know," said my husband. "We'll eat half the curry. Then we'll have sex. Then we'll have the other half of the curry." Romance is not dead in my house.

This year, we decided to up our game by having our romantic meal *outside of the house*. Which of course kicked off an argument about *where to go*.

"What about that great little place on the corner?" he said.

"No," I said. "I am not celebrating my wedding anniversary at Nando's."

"But they've got refillable Coke!" he said.

Actually, we ended up having a really nice evening. Nothing says happy anniversary like collecting your own cutlery.

Like meals out, sex takes more planning once you have kids. Our baby still sleeps in our bedroom, so we usually do it in the spare room, or as we call it now, the Sex Box.

Foreplay means hauling all the bags we keep meaning to take to the charity shop off the bed. And if we've forgotten to turn the radiator on, sex begins with me taking all my clothes off under the duvet while shouting, "JESUS, THERE'S A CHILL ON THESE SHEETS." Sends my husband from six to midnight and no mistake.

But I'm proud of us for managing to have sex, even if it is once a year, halfway through a lamb biryani, surrounded by Lidl carrier bags full of old Lee Child novels. I forget about the struggle for survival as I'm reminded that we're still us, we're still together, and for those eight minutes, that's the only thing that matters.

QUIZ: DID OUR HUSBANDS REALLY SAY THAT?

Having kids means entering a new phase of your relationship where you communicate with a new kind of honesty, thanks to all the tiredness and rage. Don't be surprised if your partner suddenly begins offering helpful comments about your parenting skills, appearance, or in fact your entire personality.

SCUMMY MUMMY CONFESSION

"My son once emerged from the house at a family barbecue singing into a vibrator. #notmine"

The Scummy Mummy husbands are especially good at this. Can you guess which of these statements they actually said to our faces?

1. After noticing our new glasses:
a. "I love those frames. They really accentuate your bone structure."
b. "You look like Sarah Palin."

2. In response to a complaint about looking whale-like at seven months pregnant:
a. "No babe, you're more beautiful than you've ever been."
b. "Actually, you look like a pregnant whale."

3. Ten hours into labour:
a. "You're doing great, darling. I'm so proud of you and your amazing body."
b. "Look, I'm tired too. I did a full day's work, remember?"

4. Pillow talk, following the first sex session, post-childbirth:
a. "That was wonderful. It's so great to reconnect physically."
b. "Before you had a baby, your skin was all taut and smooth, like a dolphin. Now it's sort of... spongy."

5. While walking up a hill behind us:
a. "Hey, you look great in those new jeans."
b. "BUMBA BUMBA BUMBA BUMBA... Did I say that out loud?"

6. During a visit from the in-laws:
a. "I know things are a bit tough right now, but they mean well."
b. "Would you like my mum to show you how to hang the washing out properly?"

Answers: All b). Yes, our husbands really said that.

ACTUAL TOP TIP

George McEncroe, single mum

"As we all know, relationships don't always work out. If you find yourself parenting on your own, resist the urge to compete in the Suffering Olympics. You'll always meet another single mum with more kids, less money and a shittier ex than you. Everyone is struggling – and that includes your married friends.

"If you're the one who left, avoid the people who tell you your decision was wrong. They were not there. They don't know. The tree is gone – it doesn't matter who chopped it down. It is really fucking hard, but you have to do the right thing according to your compass.

Stop talking about the break-up. This takes about 17 years, but I'm told it IS possible. Get a great therapist (don't be afraid to steal other people's.) If you can't afford that, get three really good friends and start a journal.

"Avoid booze and sentimentality and be on high alert at Christmas. Plan your time, kick shit and swear a lot. Then try to look outwards, beyond your new circumstances – it will help with the loneliness.

"You existed before him, you will exist after him, and you will be stronger, because you have to be. You will fuck it up. You will get it right. You will be OK."

TRUE STORIES: HELEN

My husband and I were together for ten years before we had kids.
So there was lots of time to travel around the world, experience new
cultures, eat exotic food and, let's be frank, get shit-faced and bonk.

How we delighted in trying out new sex positions, shagging in the
shower and doing it al fresco on a cycling holiday in Umbria. Back
in the day, a dry spell meant no sex for a whole week. This would be
followed by a weekend fuckfest, and an awkward walking gait come
Monday morning.

Sex was like a Heston Blumenthal meal, with loads of courses, a
confusing entrée involving foam, some sort of meat sculpture,
props, and a savoury dessert. These days, it's more like scoffing a
late-night kebab. It's still delicious, but there's a lot less fuss and
it's over much faster.

I've also discovered I get aroused by a whole new range of turn-
ons. Never mind ear nibbling and nipple twiddling here are some
things my husband has done that have really got my juices flowing:

1. He spontaneously washed the kitchen floor.
2. He shared half his chicken burger with me,
   even though he was drunk.
3. He did some work for Clarins and brought
   home a big bag of face creams.
4. He surprised me with a whole wheel of brie from Aldi.
5. He cleaned out the lint drawer in the tumble dryer.

But it's taken a while to enter this new phase of our erotic lives.
In the early days of parenthood, I wasn't thinking about sex.
I was too busy worrying whether we'd ever talk to each other again
without starting each sentence: "Oh for fuck's sake..." Underneath
all the shouting, sighing and hissed insults, there was a sense of
mourning for our forgotten friendship, sense of humour and love.

It was a while before we had sex for the first time after the baby was born – nine months, in fact. This seemed about right: nine months of pregnancy, followed by nine months of abstinence to let my foo-foo recover.

We were on a mini-break in France. The baby was asleep in the room next door, and we were just lying there, holding hands in the dark. Maybe it was the carafe of rosé, maybe it was the crème brûlée, but suddenly I felt it was time to reconnect.

I can't say I wasn't anxious. My poor old fanny had been through a lot in the past year and I was still breastfeeding. I had heard stories about lactating women whose milk jugs exploded at the point of climax. I mean, I'm no prude, but I wasn't up for role-playing a fire hydrant. But despite a nervous start, it was really lovely, and I managed not to cover either of us in milk.

That was seven years ago, and we've gone on to have sex at least eight more times since then. Parenting has got easier, too. I know our relationship will never be the same, because intimacy and foreplay mean different things now. In the old days, I'd stare lovingly into my hubby's eyes after a night of shagging, never wanting to let him go. Now I get that feeling from lying on the sofa after a day of child-wrangling, watching him call the curry house while folding laundry. Basically, random acts of kindness and moments of love mean more than a drunken fumble under the duvet.

Romance hasn't died. It was feeling a bit peaky for a while, but it's perked up and swapped hearts and flowers for Play-Doh and spaghetti hoops. And that's OK by me.

BUMPS, BIRTH AND BODILY FLUIDS: AND SO IT BEGINS

If hell is other people, then when you're pregnant, hell is other parents. As soon as you announce your forthcoming arrival, there is a queue of people lining up to give you advice.

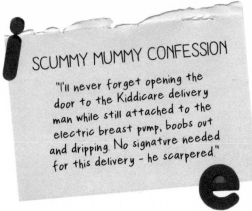

"Of course, you can't possibly prepare yourself for having a child," they say, before listing 75 ways you need to prepare yourself for having a child.

They always round off with a wry smile and a shake of the head, adding, "You've no idea what you're letting yourself in for" – oblivious to the fact that you do have some idea, having just spent two hours listening to them talk about it.

If there's one thing new parents don't need, apart from a special nappy bin that costs more to run than a small car, it's more advice. But there are some things we do wish we'd known before we had babies.

Firstly, your life is not over. The way some people talk, you'd think having a baby means never sleeping, going down the pub, or having sex again. This is not true! One of us had sex just last June.

Not every parent feels that huge rush of love at the moment of birth, like you see in the movies. Don't panic if the only thought that pops into your head the first time you see your baby is: "He looks a bit like Michael Gambon." The love will come.

This goes for fathers, too. Lots of dads seem to expect the arrival of their first child to be something like the start of *The Lion King*, except with fewer giraffes. Try not to be disappointed if things don't work out like that.

But if there's one piece of advice we'd like to offer above all others, it's this: ignore all advice. Every baby is different, and so is every parent. You'll find out what works for you. Don't be afraid to ask for help, and don't worry. You'll be fine.

And P.S., you won't BELIEVE how loud babies' farts are.

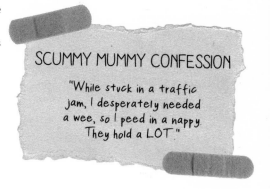

SCUMMY MUMMY CONFESSION

"While stuck in a traffic jam, I desperately needed a wee, so I peed in a nappy. They hold a LOT."

FANTASY VS REALITY: HAVING A BABY

When pregnant with your first child, you might find yourself idly daydreaming about what life with your new baby will be like. And of course there's lots of love, joy and fun to look forward to. But it's not quite one big Pampers ad, as this handy table demonstrates.

Fantasy	Reality
You will spend your third trimester wafting around in a serene haze. Strangers will compliment you on your shiny hair and radiant skin while being blinded by your wondrous glow.	You will sweat like a pig in a fur coat as your ankles swell to the size and shape of Christmas hams. You will spend the last three weeks sitting on a haemorrhoids doughnut, necking Gaviscon while your husband reluctantly clips your toenails.
The birth will be an amazing, sensuous experience. You will breathe through each contraction like the powerful warrior woman you are, feeling no pain, just rushes of ecstasy and bliss.	No.
You will be totally prepared to bring the baby home, having filled the freshly painted nursery with tiny teddies, cashmere blankets, colour-coordinated nasal aspirators, and baby-wipe warmers.	You will realise within 24 hours of getting home that you're going to need another 400 muslin squares.

Your baby will be dressed in gorgeous matching separates designed by Jools Oliver. You will sport a coordinating Breton top, ballet flats and maybe some dungarees, to show you're still fun and on trend.

You will endlessly rotate the four supermarket babygros that don't have crap poppers or too many obvious stains. You will live in yoga pants and forget what bras are for.

Daily life will be an endless whirl of baby pilates classes, swimming lessons, Sing & Sign sessions and sipping lattes in cafés as you discuss the joy of motherhood with your new mum friends.

You will count any day you manage to put shoes on as a good day. You will meet your new mum friends in the pub and spend the whole time bitching about how useless your respective partners are.

SCUMMY MUMMY CONFESSION

"I overheard my son's friend telling him he was born in the hospital. 'I was born at home,' my son replied. 'My mum couldn't be bothered going to hospital.'"

TRUE STORIES: ELLIE

There were no scented candles at the birth of my first baby.
No classical music, no yogic breathing. The only sound, apart
from me swearing, came from a radio someone had left on in the
delivery room, which was playing Bon Jovi's *Livin' on a Prayer*.
"Take my hand," said my husband. "We'll make it, I swear." He will
never play the piano again.

I have huge respect for women who give birth at home, and I'm
glad it's an ever more acceptable option. But I knew it wasn't right
for me. I feel safe in hospitals, and I have no issues with 'sterile
environments'. To me, that just means clean, which is appealing to
someone who hasn't hoovered under the bed since we moved in.

At around 14 hours, my first labour was relatively short, although it
didn't feel it at the time. It was tough going as the baby was back-
to-back. In the end they had to pull him out with the sink plunger,
and give me an episiotomy. I never thought having my fanny sliced
open would feel like a mercy, but it's funny how things turn out.

My favourite bit was afterwards, when the midwife covered my
boobs with a towel – "For your modesty." I explained I thought it
was a bit late for that, pointing to the man with his face between my
legs, sewing up my minge.

The big shock for me, though, wasn't the pain of childbirth, or even
the struggle of having a newborn – we were living with my parents
at the time, so I was fortunate enough to have a huge amount of
support. But I wasn't prepared for what I like to call The Fear.

The Fear is what wakes you up to check your baby is still breathing
six times a night. The Fear is what overrides the part of you that
knows it's nappy rash and makes you spend hours Googling
'childhood leprosy'. The Fear feels like the price you pay for
happiness; it's the constant worry that it could all disappear, at any
moment, with a single careless oversight, or a simple twist of fate.

I spent the first few weeks of my baby's life simultaneously overwhelmed with joy and consumed with terror. Not just of something terrible happening to my son, but of feeling like this for the rest of my life: of never being able to truly relax again.

I wish I had talked to someone about it. And I wish that person had said to me: "Don't worry. You will always be afraid for your son, because you will always love him. But you will learn to live with The Fear. It will quieten down. It will become manageable, and sometimes even useful. Now shut up and drink this enormous glass of Merlot."

But blimey, if I thought The Fear was bad then, I had no idea what was coming. My second baby arrived nine weeks early, most likely due to a bout of norovirus I'd suffered a few days previously. They whipped him out via an emergency Caesarean, and it was all a bit of a blur. I mainly remember telling my husband to turn the radio off this time ("I can't give birth to the fucking Eagles, man"), and the doctors discussing the season finale of *Homeland* as they sewed me up. "Hey guys: spoilers!"

The reality of having a premature baby didn't really hit me until the next day, when the morphine wore off and I saw him in his little plastic box. He spent six weeks in hospital and it was the worst time of my life. But he got well, we got through it, and now he is a gorgeous, happy, bouncy little boy. So is my eldest, despite the sink plunger thing. If anything, his head is less pointy than his father's.

As we're told so often, every birth is unique, and so is every baby. Mums are different, too, which is why I think we should all be allowed to have a say in the kind of labour we want.

One thing we have in common, though, is that we'd do anything for our kids, and that starts with pushing them out of a hole that feels like it wasn't designed for this sort of thing. Good job it's worth it.

THE RIGHT-ON DADS ON: CHILDBIRTH

Hey, guys. Rod and Rod here, proud hipster dads. Now let's keep it real – childbirth is one of the hardest things you can do, like ending climate change, or making gnocchi from scratch. And that goes for guys just as much as women. We may not have vaginas, but we have feelings, too. So here are our top tips for getting through labour, based on our extensive experience.

Bring the Essentials
Don't forget to pack a special manbag to take to hospital with you. Pop in some goji berries for energy, your favourite vinyl LPs, any knitting you're working on, some earplugs, a blindfold and a trusted beard trimmer.

Turn It Up to Eleven
Make sure you have an extra TENS machine for yourself. Give your partner the controller and hook it up to your testicles. That way, every time she has a contraction, she can press the button and you can share the moment.

Pool Your Resources
Birthing pools are great for relaxation. Don't be afraid to jump in and do a few laps.

Show Your Feelings
Birth can be a really emotional experience for men, so know that it's OK to cry during the labour. Or the third trimester. Or the entire pregnancy. Or the conception. In fact, one of us cried so hard at the hospital they had to put us on a drip for dehydration.

SCUMMY MUMMY CONFESSION
"I was throwing my seven month-old into the air to make him laugh, smiling widely to encourage him. He vomited straight into my open mouth. Didn't taste too bad."

Strike a Cord

The midwife will probably have a lot to do; keep reminding her you want to be the one who cuts the cord so she doesn't forget. If you want to keep it really real, show your partner you understand the primal nature of the experience she's been through by using your teeth.

Afterbirth Thoughts

Make sure you preserve that placenta. Fry it up with some peppers for a tasty post-birth burrito, or why not turn it into pâté? This makes an ideal dish to serve at the baby's naming ceremony, and everyone will be really surprised when they find out what they've been eating.

If you don't want to go down the conventional route, try freeze-drying the placenta. Then you can use it in craft projects, or turn it into potpourri.

You're welcome, guys. If you'd like to learn more about our experiences of labour, do check out our new ebook: *Canoeing down the Vaginal Canal: Journey to the Centre of the Birth.*

ACTUAL TOP TIP

Clemmie Hooper, midwife and author of *How to Grow a Baby and Push It Out*

"When it comes to choosing what kind of birth to have, keep your options and your mind open. Birth changes, and you can't control many aspects of it, but staying calm works wonders. Do your research and consider some kind of hypnobirthing – breathing, visualisation and so on. It can really make a difference.

"One of the things I'm asked most often is whether everyone shits themselves. No, they don't, but we love a poo, us midwives! It means the baby is coming, and you're pushing in the right place. We need to get over the pooing thing – it's not worth worrying about.

"If you want to give your midwife a gift, no chocolates or hand cream, thanks, as we get loads. Great presents I've been given include a lovely bottle of wine, a gorgeous candle and a massage treatment. But the best things I've ever received are the handwritten cards with photos. I've kept every single one."

TOP FIVE GAMES TO PLAY WITH YOUR MUMS' GROUP

Becoming a mum can be a shock to the system. Time for socialising gets shorter as your boobs grow longer, while your circle of friends widens along with your vagina.

Joining a mums' group such as the NCT is a good way to meet people who are going through the same things as you, and also enjoy whinging about them. Those first meetings can be a little awkward, though, with everyone trying to be as nice as possible while secretly plotting to murder anyone who nicks the name they've chosen for their baby.

So here are some ice-breaker games to get everyone laughing and swearing, instead of comparing the turning circles of the Bugaboo Cameleon and the Maclaren Globetrotter.

1. Handbag Surprise
A Scummy Mummies classic. Each mum takes it in turn to pull something revolting out of her handbag. Typical examples include half-sucked lollipops, dirty socks and old nappies. The owner of the scummiest item wins the jackpot – all the other scummy items!

2. Hands or Tits?
Aural fun. Everyone in the group closes their eyes apart from one person, who makes a clapping noise. The rest of the group has to guess whether they created that sound using their hands or their boobs. This is a great opener – nothing quite breaks the ice like shouting "TITS" in the face of a woman you hardly know.

3. Gin for Jeans
Each player gets a pen and a piece of paper. Everyone has to write down the date they last washed their jeans. The person who has left it the longest wins a bottle of gin.

4. CSI: Mymummy
All mums are covered in mystery stains at all times. The game here is to guess the origins of the stains on each other's clothing, handbag, buggy, etc. Each time one is correctly identified, the entire group must sing: "Poooooo are you? Poo-poo, poo-poo" to

the tune of the *CSI* theme song. Yes, you are grown women. But you are also mothers, so you might as well get used to the idea of finding poo hilarious.

5. Scum Dine with Me

A multiple-choice quiz. Each player lists three disgusting meals – two they have made up and one they have actually eaten. The rest of the group has to guess which one is real. As an example, here are our dirty dinners:

HELEN

A
The remains of a pizza the children have already chewed the toppings off

B
A whole packet of Cheestrings

C
One of those microwave burgers, unmicrowaved

ELLIE

A
A Fray Bentos Steak & Ale Pie with a side order of Monster Munch

B
An entire gratin made with 1kg potatoes and 2 pints cream

C
Leftover curry eaten cold, straight out of the tin, in the bath

(This is sort of a trick question as we have eaten all these things, but you get the idea.)

TRUE STORIES: HELEN

As a Scummy Mummy, most of my parenting decisions are based around what requires the least amount of effort, fuss and time away from my own sofa. So giving birth at home felt like the logical choice for me. I knew there were no guarantees things would go according to plan, but I liked the idea of coughing out a baby in my lounge, then going back to bed with a mug of tea and a Terry's Chocolate Orange.

As births go, I was dealt a good hand – or more specifically, I was given wide hips and an elastic fanny. I loved being at home, with my scented candles and my classical music. Frankly, it was more romantic and pleasant than a lot of dates I've been on. Apart from the bit at the end, when I pooed myself in front of three women I didn't know.

I remember my waters breaking quite clearly. I was watching a show about former MP John Prescott and laughing so hard that initially I thought I'd just wet my pants. I still think it's hilarious that John Prescott sent me into labour...

My husband reacted by running round in circles while looking panic-stricken, which was of course very helpful and relaxing. I tried to stay positive, but despite six months of yoga and breathing training, that first contraction hit me hard.

A few hours later, just as I was getting used to the sensation of a watermelon trying to pop itself out of my front bottom, I entered 'transition'. It's called that because you transition from deep breathing while being grateful for the midwife rubbing your back and hubby holding your hand, to screaming: "GET ME TO THE FUCKING HOSPITAL AND GET ME SOME FUCKING DRUGS NOW, YOU MASSIVE BUNCH OF ARSEHOLES."

By dawn, I had lost the power of speech and was mooing like a cow. I tried using the TENS machine but this seemed to make the contractions worse, so I decided it wasn't the right birthing choice for me (i.e. I threw it across the room so hard it shattered into a thousand pieces).

It was around this time my husband reminded me that he was really tired too, having done a full day's work before I went into labour. This was not a high point of our marriage.

After that I had a bit of a float in the inflatable pool. The pushing part was still intense, but I got through it by crushing all the bones in Will's hands. Being on all fours helped, not least because there were a couple of incidents that required the use of a sieve, and I was pleased not to see the results. I did regret eating lamb shanks the night before.

When the head crowned, the midwife told me to put my hands down and catch the baby. With one big push, a twist and a turn, I pulled her out of the water and held her in my arms. She came out big, purple and amazing. She was definitely alive and well, as she proceeded to demonstrate by screaming for 15 minutes.

Then it was time for stage three: my husband cut the cord, I hopped out of the pool, and the midwives popped a Tesco carrier bag on the floor. The placenta flopped out with a final push. I have never felt so glamorous in my life.

After the midwives had gone, there we were, the three of us, left to stare at each other as we wondered what would happen next. We were parents. We were a family. And we have pretty much stayed together on our sofa ever since.

TIME-SAVING TIPS FOR NEW PARENTS

The first year with your baby can be challenging, what with all the sleep deprivation, nappy changing and photos you need to post on Facebook. So here are some easy ways to save time and energy.

SCUMMY MUMMY CONFESSION

"I once licked my daughter's face clean because I didn't have any baby wipes."

Give Yourself a 'Festival Shower'

Actual showers are time-consuming, and can feel pointless if you're going to get sick in your hair anyway. So why not just give yourself a once-over with some baby wipes? That way you can get (relatively) clean without leaving the sofa. Bonus tip: keep a packet in every room until your kids are at least 25.

Throw Cereal Straight on the Floor

Let's be honest: when it comes to weaning, most of the food ends up under the table or in your kid's ear. Cut out the middleman by chucking your Rice Krispies directly onto the floor.

Make Coffee the Night Before

Smart mums know they're going to drink their coffee cold anyway. So save time in the mornings by brewing your coffee at midnight, when you've finally finished all your evening chores (spent three hours on Instagram.)

SCUMMY MUMMY CONFESSION

"I always used more baby powder than necessary in the hope of creating a baby fart volcano."

Always Look 'Made-up'

Draw your make-up directly onto your face with a Sharpie for a precise look that lasts a long time. Or why not try drawing pupils onto your eyelids? This will create a handy optical illusion for the next time you fall asleep mid-conversation with a friend.

Set a Strict Door Policy

It's lovely to have lots of visitors, but make it clear they won't be allowed across the threshold unless they're carrying food and/or alcohol. In short: no lasagne, no entry. And don't let people outstay their welcome. Invest in a massive *Countdown*-style clock so they know when it's time to go. But don't let them leave until they've put their own mug in the dishwasher.

SCUMMY MUMMY CONFESSION

"I once found myself stranded in a loo, with the baby in a sling and no toilet paper. So I used the baby's sock. FUN"

SCUMMY MUMMY CONFESSIONS
SPECIAL EDITION: TIREDNESS

Being tired takes on a whole new meaning when you become a parent. In fact, if anyone without kids suggests they might be feeling a little weary themselves, you may find yourself screaming:

"YOU'RE NOT TIRED! YOU'VE NEVER BEEN TIRED IN YOUR LIFE! YOU WOULDN'T KNOW TIREDNESS IF IT WOKE YOU UP EVERY TWO HOURS, WET THE BED FOUR TIMES A NIGHT, AND INFORMED YOU IT WAS TIME TO START THE DAY BY SMACKING YOU IN THE FACE WITH A DUPLO FIRE ENGINE AT 5AM!"

Or at least that's what you shout in your head, because you're too exhausted to vocalise more than three words at a time.

There's even scientific research showing the tiredness you experience from looking after a baby has the same effect on your brain as being drunk. It's a lot less fun, of course, and you're less likely to end up dancing on the table while singing *Love Shack*, but you will still pass out on the sofa at the end of the night.

Tiredness is such a big issue for parents that it's one of the most popular topics for Scummy Mummy Confessions. So here's a bumper selection of our favourites.

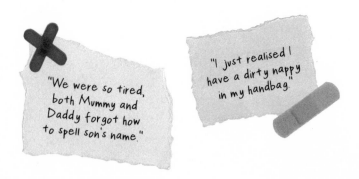

"We were so tired, both Mummy and Daddy forgot how to spell son's name."

"I just realised I have a dirty nappy in my handbag."

"I used to pee in the bin in between breastfeeding at night, so I didn't have to leave the baby and go downstairs."

"Before he learned how to blow it himself, I used to suck snot out of Sebastian's nose."

"When my first son was four weeks old, he slept through the night for the first time, and I didn't wake up to change his nappy. In the morning, I found a blister on his bottom. Wracked with guilt, I rushed him to the doctor. It was my contact lens."

"I used to breastfeed when the Health Visitor came round, knowing there was formula in the fridge."

"We forgot our five-day-old baby daughter when viewing a property. The estate agent came chasing us down the street, carrying her in her car seat."

43

NAVIGATING NUTRITION: DO FISH FINGERS COUNT AS ONE OF YOUR FIVE-A-DAY?

These days there's a lot of talk about how important it is to eat well and stay in shape. Well, if you're a Scummy Mummy, that shape is spherical.

Honestly, who has time to skin chicken breasts when you're dealing with chickenpox? For those of us with small children, 'clean eating' means 'using a plate that's been rinsed under the tap'. And buying 'locally sourced' food involves grabbing a bag of oven chips from the Tesco Metro up the road.

It all starts with breastfeeding... Suddenly how, what and where you're feeding your child are everybody's business. The food you eat becomes a topic for discussion, too. Breastfeeding mums are told to avoid everything from chillies ("too spicy") and onions ("too gassy") to fizzy drinks ("They will make your milk fizzy" – yes, someone really said this).

Once the baby starts eating solids, and producing them, there's a whole new set of issues to deal with. How much should they be eating? Should you try baby-led weaning? What is sago, anyway? You'll spend hours mashing carrots and puréeing butternut squash, only to see it splattered about until the kitchen looks like it's been repainted in new Farrow & Ball shade, 'Miserable Sunset'.

SCUMMY MUMMY CONFESSION

"Had several kids for a play date. Scraped all the leftover pasta into a large dish, topped with grated cheese, popped it under the grill and served to unsuspecting husband."

46

But don't limit your kids to trying out their interior design skills at home; why not take them to a restaurant? There's nothing quite like trying to eat a three-course meal in 20 minutes, in between wiping hummus off the walls

before the waiter notices. And then paying £60 for the privilege.

Watch out, too, for the huffy-puffy couple without kids at the next table, tutting loudly as they judge you for letting your children have an iPad in a restaurant. (Top tip: if they get really huffy, take away the iPad, and let them enjoy the kids loudly asking where poo comes from while repeatedly knocking their cutlery on the floor.)

In an ideal world, we'd all have children who love munching on brown rice and kelp. In reality, you're probably going to spend more time than you'd like cooking chicken nuggets the exact colour and shape of Donald Trump's hair.

As children grow, their tastes change, and they do stop throwing shit around. Until then, accept the fact that most meals are going to be a bit of a chimps' tea party, and resign yourself to cleaning up the mess. Or just buy all the paper plates in the pound shop and cover your carpets in cling film.

TRUE STORIES: ELLIE

I've always been into food. Before I had kids, I spent hours lovingly preparing a three-course banquet, then I ate it while reading a cookbook and planning my next meal. My husband said this was like watching porn while having sex. Which is nonsense, obviously. Food is much better than sex. And who needs porn when you've got *Saturday Kitchen*?

After I had my first baby, I had much less time, energy and money to spend on food. I found myself involuntarily on what I like to call the New Mum Diet. Here's a typical meal plan:

BREAKFAST Two swigs of a cup of tea hastily made by husband while getting ready for work. Rest of tea abandoned following distraction in the form of dirty nappy / Amazon delivery / phone call from health visitor / burning smell coming from dishwasher etc. Pattern to be repeated throughout the day, until entire house is dotted with cold cups of tea, as if they are mating.

LUNCH Hummus and carrot sticks. Not because it's a healthy choice, but because it's the cheapest thing on the menu at the chic hipster café where your rich new NCT friend suggested meeting. Still costs only slightly less than a new pair of shoes.

AFTERNOON SNACK Desperately rummage in cupboard for chocolate digestives, only to remember you ate the whole packet in one go yesterday, to get over having opened the door to the postman with your boob out. Squirt some tomato ketchup on a cracker instead.

DINNER Husband arrives home to find you slaving over a hot stove (boiling the kettle for pasta.) You watch him think about pointing out you've had pesto spaghetti four nights in a row. You glance casually at the knife block. He backs slowly out of the room.

But although the quality of my diet diminished when I had a baby, my love for food grew even stronger. Instead of just being about pleasure, it became about comforting myself in hard times, and rewarding myself for getting through them.

More than once, I found myself sitting in supermarket car park, baby in the back, gnawing on a ham knuckle from the hot food counter. Often at 9.30AM. Passers-by would stare in horror as I tore at the bones with my teeth, fat dripping down my chin. I must have looked like some sort of starving cavewoman, recently escaped from the Natural History Museum in a Honda Civic.

But I didn't care. Chowing down on all that fatty, salty goodness felt like more than just a treat. It was compensation for having been up breastfeeding all night. It was the source of the energy I'd need to get through the rest of the day. Most of all, it was about the stolen moment, about doing something that was just for me. For at least a few minutes until it was time for the baby's next feed, when I'd cover both him and the steering wheel in pork fat.

Now the children are a bit older, we eat together as a family most nights (which sounds lovely and wholesome, except there are lots of chicken nuggets and frozen pizzas involved). But some evenings, I still like to bung the kids some beans on toast, then cook something grown-up after they've gone to bed.

I love a bit of quiet chopping and stirring, with Radio 4 on and a glass of wine at my elbow. It's my time to relax and let go of the stresses of the day, without anyone asking me for anything. When you've spent 12 hours explaining why wheels are round and where Peru is, even "How was your day?" can feel like a question too far.

Then there's the satisfaction of sitting down to a proper meal, full of things like capers and anchovies. We get to eat while watching grown-up TV, and sometimes we have a conversation. Now and then, feeling content, calm and full of wine, we have sex afterwards. He rarely notices I've got half an eye on *Celebrity MasterChef*.

THE SCUMMY MUMMIES FIVE-A-DAY

Getting most small children to eat five portions of healthy goodness a day is close to impossible, unless you class jam as a fruit.

Left to their own devices, kids would probably subsist on a diet of things like sand, Transformers stickers and torn-up napkins. So if your child eats mostly food-like substances from any category, you are winning.

As for your own diet, there's no point trying to keep to a strict macrobiotic regime. Alfalfa sprouts and tofu will not give you the energy you need for chasing a screaming toddler round a soft-play centre. This is about survival, so don't feel bad if some days you end up breakfasting on digestives, enjoying a light lunch of Mini Babybels and finishing up with gin for dinner.

Here's the Scummy Mummies guide to what you and your child will probably end up eating every day – because you live in the real world.

CHILDREN'S FIVE-A-DAY

Something salty

Something fried

Something off the floor

Something in a small packet

A Fruit Shoot

MUM'S FIVE-A-DAY

Carbs (crusts, cold pizza, Weetabix)

More carbs (pasta, crisps, Hobnobs)

Something that has been previously chewed

Cheese

Wine

ACTUAL TOP TIP

**Jo Travers, registered dietitian and founder of
The London Nutritionist**

"Fish fingers are brilliant. They tick so many boxes:
nutritious, convenient, not expensive and kids love them.
But beware, they are not all created equally! Some are
loaded with salt, or are made out of minced fish –
what's left over when when all the best bits have been
used for other things, stuck together with goodness
knows what.

"Price isn't always an indicator of quality, so read
the ingredients list. Cod is no better than pollock,
nutritiously speaking (and is often over-fished), so don't
feel you need to shell out extra for this. Serve with a
vegetable and some carbs for a well-balanced meal."

THE RIGHT-ON DADS ON: CLEAN EATING

Hey, guys. As Right-on Dads, we spend a lot of time thinking about what we put in our mouths. We're massive gourmets, and we believe food is literally the food of life.

Obviously, it has to be organic, and locally sourced. And you can't get much more local than our back garden. We're pretty much self-sufficient now; we only pop down to the shops for the essential stuff you just can't grow at home – things like capers, tapenade and lettuce.

We love to cook, especially for special occasions. You won't find any Fruit Shoots at our kids' birthday parties – you might as well give your child a tin of treacle and a ladle, or some heroin. We like to offer gluten-free fairy cakes made entirely from Medjool dates and agave nectar, and a bespoke wicker piñata filled with hummus. It's wonderful to watch the kids going at it with their little breadsticks.

Obviously, we don't really celebrate Christmas, because of all the commercialism, religiosity and excessive fun. But we do like to cook a big meal for our families to celebrate the Winter Solstice on 25 December. Our favourite recipes include pig's anus panettone, and that thing Yotam Ottolenghi does with turkey and Iranian kumquats. (Top tip, guys: don't worry if you run out of ricotta and pomegranate molasses, like we did one year; just substitute with Dairylea and Ribena.)

When it comes to everyday cooking, we're with Jamie Oliver – there's no excuse not to produce a healthy meal from scratch every night while simultaneously hanging out the washing, running a bath,

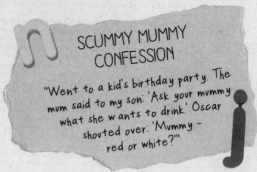

SCUMMY MUMMY CONFESSION

"Went to a kid's birthday party. The mum said to my son: 'Ask your mummy what she wants to drink.' Oscar shouted over: 'Mummy – red or white?'"

breastfeeding and practising phonics, as we keep explaining to our wives.

The key to success is stocking your larder with versatile ingredients like spelt flour and small brown lentils. Dried chickpeas are also excellent – they're cheap, they have a long shelf life, and they enable you to prepare a tasty, nutritious meal in less than 14 hours.

You don't need expensive gadgets to eat healthily, so put that microwave in the bin and get an Aga. Another great tip is to buy yourself, or your partner, a spiraliser. They are superb for making fresh, healthy veg taste like soggy wool. You can spiralise pretty much anything – courgettes, celeriac, spaghetti, butter... And if you have any spiralised noodles left over, why not try knitting your own vegan gilet?

We're big fans of slow cooking and love to spend whole Sundays in the kitchen, prepping a delicious roadkill and nettle tagine while our wives keep an eye on the kids. We believe you shouldn't be afraid to get your hands, or the kitchen, dirty – the more pans and utensils you use, the better the chef you are. And the great news is that because you cooked, you don't have to clean up!

So there you go, guys. Clean eating isn't just about washing your veg – it's about making the right choices. And then telling everyone about them.

SCUMMY MUMMY
CONFESSION

"I fed my child a chocolate coin sandwich for tea."

TRUE STORIES: HELEN

What your kid eats, or doesn't eat, can be one of the most soul-destroying challenges of early parenthood. I adore all food, so I assumed my children would be the same, happily gobbling up pickled herring and olives washed down with mineral water. However, as with most things about parenting, I was wrong.

The term 'fussy eater' gets thrown around all the time. Usually by older, well-meaning relatives, who use it as code for 'your son's a little shit'.

Another phrase I hear a lot is, "What, he doesn't eat pasta?" followed by: "But all kids love pasta!" They do not. I have five years of research to back this up, along with 17 discarded packets of dried fusilli.

I know the theory – children will politely eat whatever they're served, if they're hungry enough. That's what my mum and all the books promised me. In reality, I start to feel the waves of panic at about 5PM each day. I look in the fridge for answers (as I do when faced with most problems). If I'm lucky, I will find some sausages, meatballs, or pizza. More likely, I will weep at the sight of half a shrivelled lemon and a rock-hard crumpet.

I've tried hiding grated courgettes in a meal, sculpting carrots into the shape of Peppa Pig and all that stuff: it doesn't work. The only solution is to calm myself down with a glass of wine and get out the Weetabix. After all, it's carbs, isn't it? Just like pasta.

"Kids, we're having cereal for dinner! It's upside-down day!"

"Hurray! We love you, Mummy!"

It wasn't always this way. My kids ate most things until they learned to talk and the word "NO." My son was corrupted on a trip to France when he was about 14 months old. We were staying in one of those all-inclusive hotels and he was presented with mounds of croissants for breakfast and baskets of baguettes for lunch.

"What harm could it do?" we told ourselves, over yet more glasses of wine. "Living off wheat for a few days won't kill him. When we get home he'll be back on the broccoli purée, no worries." But we had allowed our son to enter a world where all food is beige, and he never came back.

So you could say it's all our fault, but personally, I like to blame France.

Since he started school, the range of foods my son will eat has expanded to include fruit (bananas, but only if there are no brown bits) and vegetables (potatoes). But I still feel the fear whenever he's off on a play date, and the other mum breezily says she'll give him dinner. I know her lovingly prepared spag bol or pesto penne will go untouched while my son hides under the table, or on one particularly memorable occasion, closes his eyes and puts his fist in his mouth.

Eating out is stressful, too. I dream of the day we can have a meal in a restaurant that isn't Pizza Express or McDonald's. But it's not all bad – I do really like dough balls.

And I am reassured by advice from older parents who've been through this already: "Don't worry, my child ate nothing but ketchup sandwiches for five years. Now she's a human rights lawyer!"

I remind myself of this as I'm serving my son another meal of sliced white bread with a side order of breadsticks and a mashed potato garnish. One day, I tell myself, he will achieve world peace. Even better, he might eat something green.

SURVIVAL GUIDE: FOOD SHOPPING

Back in prehistoric times, hunter-gatherers had it easy. Who wouldn't rather wrestle a sabre-toothed tiger than to drag a four-year-old round Sainsbury's on a wet Wednesday afternoon?

But there are ways to make the whole experience a little easier. Here's the Scummy Mummies guide to surviving your weekly shop.

Be Prepared
Don't leave for the supermarket without packing the essentials:

Know the Terrain
Think of the supermarket as a war zone. Avoid minefields (the sweet and toy aisles) and booby traps (two-for-one offers on Pom-Bears). Keep your head down, and keep your troops (children) in order using strict military discipline (threats and bribes).

☐	car keys
☐	wallet
☐	carrier bags
☐	shopping list
☐	trolley coin
☐	baby wipes
☐	change of clothes
☐	toys
☐	Valium
☐	lasso
☐	butterfly net
☐	tranquiliser gun
☐	
☐	
☐	
☐	

Never Show Weakness
Kids aren't the only ones susceptible to temptation in the supermarket, but you must be strong. If you start loading the trolley with brie and discount wine, you'll find it much harder to say no to that six-pack of Thomas the Tank Engine pasta shapes. Things can get even tougher if you're in a discount supermarket, but ask yourself: do you really NEED a foot spa? Or a gigantic tin of Quality Street? (Actually, if you have just survived food shopping with kids, maybe you do.)

Ignore Your Friends

It's great to bump into your neighbour or that nice mum from Book Club, but don't stop to chat or your child will take this as a cue to start systematically emptying the shelves. If you see someone you know, just shout "FACEBOOK ME!" while running away. Better still, wear a fake beard and moustache so no one will recognise you.

Engage in Criminal Acts

We're not talking actual shoplifting here. But sometimes the only way to get through a supermarket trip is by distracting your children with food you haven't yet paid for. Don't feel bad about it – Lord Sainsbury can surely spare a handful of grapes, and Mr Tesco won't miss that cheeky Peperami, or the odd rotisserie chicken.

Embrace Technology

Alternatively, fuck that shit and order it all online.

ACTUAL TOP TIP

Helen McGinn, wine expert and author of
The Knackered Mother's Wine Club

"When it comes to matching food and wine, there are lots of classics. Oysters and Muscadet, say. Or sushi and Champagne. All very well, but if the staple seafood in your diet is leftover fish fingers, what should you go for?

"Not just whatever's open; anything too light and the wine will be lost (a terrible waste). Too heavy and you won't be able to taste the fish fingers (not so bad). A medium-bodied white like a simple Mâcon Villages (that's the Chardonnay grape) works, as does a simple, fresh Provence rosé. Or go for a lightish red, like a juicy Spanish Tempranillo. So many wines, so little time..."

POTTY TRAINING, PUSHCHAIRS AND PEPPA PIG: DEALING WITH THE DAILY GRIND

Having a baby can feel like being in the trenches. The good news is that once your child gets a bit older, things start to settle down. It's more like living in an occupied territory run by a despotic overlord, one who's obsessed with *Octonauts* and rice cakes.

Every aspect of life requires a different approach. Planning a holiday is no longer a question of booking a last-minute mini-break. It requires the same amount of forethought, equipment and money as it takes to traverse a polar ice cap.

Expect your home to be transformed once you've had kids. It's as if you've been caught in a hurricane and woken up in some shit version of Oz. Everything is brightly coloured, there are lots of small people and you may be accompanied by a man who lacks courage and brains.

Your car will basically turn into a bin on wheels, and your clothes will magnetically attract food and bodily fluids. Your social life will become a series of play dates and park trips, and you will learn there is no more wretched hive of scum and villainy than a soft play on a rainy Saturday.

SCUMMY MUMMY CONFESSION

"Hubby came home to find me crying on the floor in the corner of the bathroom, with poo in my hair. 'Potty training is FINISHED.'"

The fact is, everyday life is different when you have a baby – in all the ways you expected, and many more you didn't. But along with all the hard stuff, there are plenty of fun surprises, lovely moments and opportunities to have a good laugh. And it's great to get past the sleepless nights and stress of having a newborn. At least until you decide to have another one...

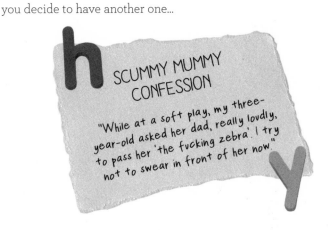

SCUMMY MUMMY
CONFESSION

"While at a soft play, my three-year-old asked her dad, really loudly, to pass her 'the fucking zebra'. I try not to swear in front of her now."

SCUMMY MUMMY LIFE HACKS

Life with small children isn't always one big Boden catalogue, especially if you're scummy. So here are our top tips for getting through the day.

Avoid That Awkward 'Are you Pregnant?' Conversation
Have you got a tummy that confuses friends, family and fellow commuters? Upcycle that 'Baby On Board' badge with a Sharpie. Try crossing out the word 'Baby' and replacing with 'Cheese'. Or keep it nice and simple with the phrase 'JUST FAT'. No one will ever ask how far along you are again!

Make Trousers Last Longer
Little one outgrowing those tracksuit bottoms already? Stick them in a pair of wellies. Ta-da! Good for another three months.

Days Out Don't Have to Be Pricey
Save money by taking kids to the 'free zoo', or as it's otherwise known, the pet shop. For another cheap outing, let them run wild at the 'Scandinavian-style soft play' (IKEA mattress department).

Get Yourself a Mummy Bib
Invest in a scarf – they're like muslins for mums. Great for mopping up sick, wiping noses and hiding a bad hair day. Can even be used as a nappy in an emergency.

Teach Your Kids It's Bedtime As Soon As *The Archers* Comes On
Then download the theme tune, hide the clocks and just hit play whenever you're ready for the day to end.

Teach Your Children to Call McDonald's 'the Farmers' Market'
No one will judge you if the kids loudly announce they went to the farmers' market for lunch again yesterday. For bonus points, refer to Happy Meals as 'mezze platters' and the free toys as 'falafel'.

Wine Makes Everything Better

Just pour yourself a nice, big glass (or mug, if it's still only teatime) and drink up. There now.

But Really, There's Only One Parenting Life Hack Anyone Needs: Remember to Laugh

Laughter will get you through the tears, the tantrums and the tough times. It will sustain you through disastrous day trips and marathon *Kate & Mim-Mim* sessions. Laughing with your partner will keep your relationship alive. Laughing with your kids will remind you why you had them. And laughing at yourself is a great way to remember that nobody's perfect – your best is good enough, even when it's rubbish.

SCUMMY MUMMY CONFESSION

"On a flight to Australia, I let my daughter watch telly and drink as much free juice as she liked. I thought this would give me a chance to nap. But during one particularly funny movie, she laughed so hard she weed everywhere. They had to replace the entire chair."

TRUE STORIES: ELLIE

When my youngest child was seven months old, we decided to go on a camping trip.

When some people heard this, they raised their eyebrows as if I'd just said: "We're climbing Kilimanjaro blindfolded, then racing down it on unicycles" or "We're going to IKEA on a bank holiday Monday." But I don't believe having children should stop you from doing what you want to do.

Hahaha what nonsense. What I really wanted to do was spend a week in Tuscany, lying around, drinking wine and never having to wipe anyone else's bottom. But that was not an option. Camping was all about carefree fun and wild adventure – and more to the point, cheaper.

I tried to remind myself of this on the third morning of the holiday, after another nine hours on a crap lilo with a baby who wanted feeding every two hours, having awoken to find the tent collapsing around me like a fabric coffin. I sort of wished it was one.

But it is possible to survive camping with small children. We've even found that having kids doesn't have to alter your enjoyment of festivals. (Certainly not if you're my husband, who popped out for "a few beers" one night and returned to the tent at 5.30AM covered in mud, looking insane and babbling about "this really cool chick I met who's got an Airstream". Good times.)

The trick is to be prepared, and by that I mean bring 200 packs of baby wipes and a lot of alcohol. Booze warms you up from the inside out. It makes crap lilos more comfortable and tinned food tastier. Sure, we've all seen Ben Fogle spend six hours rubbing sticks together while drinking his own wee, but once the cameras are off, I bet there's nothing he likes better than relaxing with a nice pint of Baileys. (JUST BUY A LIGHTER, FOGLE. THEY ARE FIVE FOR A POUND DOWN THE MARKET.)

But the absolute best accessory you can take along on a camping trip is an Australian. This is because Australians love camping. They are brilliant at it. I think it's partly because they are genetically coded to survive in harsh environmental conditions against all the odds, but mainly because they have all the stuff. Gazebos, head torches, fold-out dining tables, disposable barbecues... I know Helen thinks we ask her to go camping with us because of the jolly camaraderie, but really it's because of that tiny little tent she has just for keeping beer cool.

We've been camping a few times since the fabric coffin incident, and we'll go again. It really is fun, and it's worth putting up with the difficult bits for those magic moments when the kids are toasting marshmallows round the campfire, while the grown-ups take it in turns to pour box wine in each others' mouths because Ian forgot the glasses.

Obviously, though, I still buy a lottery ticket every week, in the hope that next year we can go to Center Parcs.

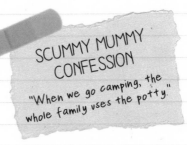

SCUMMY MUMMY
CONFESSION

"When we go camping, the whole family uses the potty."

THE RIGHT-ON DADS ON: MAN BUGGIES

 Hey, guys. It's great that there are so many cool baby products available these days – everything from sustainable bamboo potties to Mason-jar sippy cups. But us Right-On Dads have had it up to our beards with the fact that so many of these parenting aids are aimed at women!

We're big fans of equality, which is why we've created our own range of mother-and-baby products designed with men in mind. We plan to sell them in our pop-up shop in Shoreditch: JoJo Papa Bébé.

Everyone's heard of the Bugaboo, but check out our pushchair engineered especially for guys: the Buggamee. Let's take a look at those unique masculine features.

Mmm, Coffee

Most buggies come with a cup holder as standard, but we've taken that one step further. The Buggamee comes with a cafetière – just stick your freshly ground Arabica in there and off you go. But do be aware: an alarm will sound if it's not Fairtrade.

Tummy Time

Ever get peckish on the walk to Baby Capoeira Class? Don't worry – the Buggamee has a handy Mezze Shelf you can fill with all your favourite everyday snacks, like prosciutto-wrapped figs and garbanzo-bean hummus. Plus the handles are ergonomically designed so they're perfect for hanging choritho.

Nice Muff

Sheepskin pushchair liners are very popular these days, but they're no good if you're vegan. Here's our alternative, made from hand-knitted hessian. Bonus: it doubles as a gilet, so you can go straight from Toddler Gamelan Class to that Mumford & Sons concert.

Roomy Undercarriage
The Buggamee has tons of room to carry around your knitting and vinyl LPs. There's even a special pocket for just your beard trimmer.

Flying the Flags
Bunting isn't just for women, guys. Brighten up your Buggamee with some hand-crafted bunting for men, or 'munting.'

Pretty as a Picture
Show the world what a great dad you are by carrying around a photo of your kids even when you're actually with them. Or change it up – our picture frame contains a photo of Emma Watson, because she's such a great feminist.

Eco Worrier
If you're concerned about the environment – and who isn't, guys – the good news is that the Buggamee is made from entirely recycled materials. The handles are moulded out of melted down Crocs, while the tyres are made of reclaimed Hunter wellies.

Bang on Trend
The pushchair you drive should be an expression of your personality, which is why the Buggamee comes in three colourways – Burnt Wicker, Smashed Feta and our personal favourite, Taramasalatata.

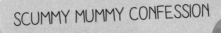

SCUMMY MUMMY CONFESSION

"My daughter needed a poo on the train. There were no toilets, so I let her do it in my friend's Tupperware box. My friend forgot, and it was in her handbag for a week."

ACTUAL TOP TIP

Tracey Davies, travel writer

"Travelling with your children is an important part of parenting. Take the nippers abroad for their holidays and you'll expand their minds, introduce them to different cultures and, hopefully, have new and wonderful experiences. The fact that it's sunny on the Continent and the booze is much cheaper are just added bonuses.

"It doesn't matter how old they are, DO NOT let your child pack their own suitcase – otherwise you could find yourself traipsing around Rome with a five-year-old dressed only in Spider-Man pants and a Kylo Ren mask. Or even a teenager attempting to make one pair of boxers last a fortnight (true story)."

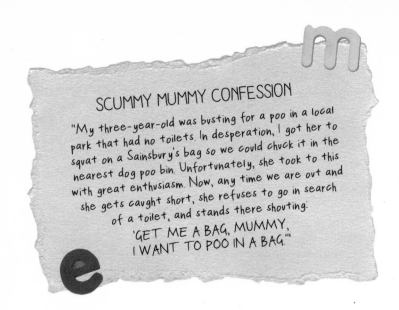

SURVIVAL GUIDE: HAVING A SECOND CHILD

The transition from one child to two can be tough. It's the difference between hosting a picnic and organising a gigantic music festival. You won't sleep much, you'll get covered in filth and you'll spend more time dealing with other people's poo and wee than you'd like.

But it doesn't have to be a complete nightmare – in fact, two kids can even be fun. It's all about being prepared. So here's our guide to what to expect when you're expecting another one.

Expect Fewer Presents
We know your precious firstborn was inundated with silver rattles, Cath Kidston bibs and handmade rocking horses from your third cousin, but don't expect the same this time around. You'll be lucky if Aunty Lynne turns up with a bottle of Cava and a packet of biscuits.

Kids' TV Is Your Friend

Your oldest will watch a lot more TV over the first year. Just accept this now. Take that rule about one episode of *SpongeBob* before bed and throw it in the bin. While you're busy feeding, changing nappies, burping and being bloody tired, stick the toddler on the sofa with Mr Tumble and some chocolate biscuits. You'll all be much happier.

Allow Two Hours to Leave the House (Minimum)

Trying to get out of the front door will take about 65 times longer than you ever imagined. So if you need to get to Sing and Sign for 11AM on Tuesday, start packing on Sunday night. (Better yet, don't bother with Sing and Sign at all. The sooner they can start asking for things, the more trouble for you.)

Here are some things that can happen when trying to leave the house with two small children:

☐	a) Getting the toddler to put their shoes, coat, gloves and/or hat on will involve actual wrestling.
☐	b) You will fail to pack at least one of the following: keys, phone, wallet, sanity.
☐	c) You will agree to take along a ridiculously large toy, just because you want to leave the house some time before midnight.
☐	d) The moment you are finally ready to walk out the door, someone will need the potty or a nappy change.
☐	e) All of the above.

Forget the Organic Kale Smoothies

The second child eats crap much earlier than the first. We know it's hard to believe now, but in 12 months' time your little one will be sucking on a chicken nugget and knocking back Haribo at a birthday party like tequila shots.

SCUMMY MUMMY
CONFESSION

"Sometimes I can't tell my twins apart in photos, so I just lie and pretend."

Here's the good news: you won't care, because your children will be happy and quiet, and someone will have just given you a glass of white wine. You must drink that wine. Just stop whatever you're doing for five minutes and Drink. That. Wine.

Say Bye-Bye to Your Boobs

Yes, right now you're prepped to breastfeed and you look like Dolly Parton. But soon those milk floats will make a beeline for your navel. Sorry. Our advice is to buy some good bras – the fancy ones, not the 'value' two-packs. You'll thank us later.

Accept Your Relationship Will Go Wonky for a Bit

We're sure your partner is a real sweetheart and super hands-on, but having a second kid puts a big strain on your relationship. There won't be as much time to sit around staring at your new baby because someone needs to make sure the first kid is alive.

You'll probably both be a bit more sweary, maybe even shouty; this is perfectly normal. When things get tough, drink some wine together and laugh at some cat videos on YouTube. This will do wonders for your relationship. We're convinced it's what's kept Posh and Becks together all this time.

Watch Out for Grandparent Fatigue

We know this sounds harsh, but the grandparents will be less interested in number two – or more specifically, looking after two kids. So expect the babysitting offers to dwindle. You'll find Nanna is suddenly busy doing the garden all the time, while Pops is tied up with his charity work (drinking in the Rotary Club bar).

Feel the Love, in a Different Way

Of course you will love your new arrival as much as you love your first. But you won't have the same amount of time or energy to devote to them. After two years of sleep deprivation, your attention to detail will be lacking. You won't mind so much if this one isn't dressed in matching Gap separates, or hasn't mastered downward-facing dog at Baby Yoga, or started talking by the age of six.

Don't worry, though – the second child will probably turn out to be more relaxed and well adjusted as a result. Just look at Prince Harry, for example. He's a HOOT!

Well, that covers everything. The thing is that life with two kids is noisy, chaotic and twice as stinky. But it's wonderful, because you also get twice the giggles, smiles and cuddles. So enjoy the gorgeous, fabulous mess your life has just become.

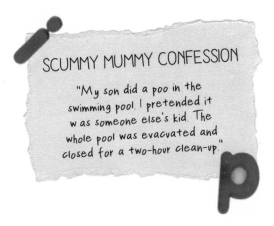

SCUMMY MUMMY CONFESSION

"My son did a poo in the swimming pool. I pretended it was someone else's kid. The whole pool was evacuated and closed for a two-hour clean-up."

TRUE STORIES: HELEN

When you become a mum, you acquire new superpowers to help you cope with some of life's most repulsive experiences. I was astonished to find I could calmly deal with a monolithic tantrum in the middle of M&S, an ear-splitting rendition of *Let It Go*, and being doused with several bodily fluids, sometimes all at once.

But there is one thing that has broken me. It has driven me to the darkest depths of despair, unleashed my rage and left me a sobbing mess. I am talking, of course, about swimming lessons.

Sure, learning to swim is an important life skill, like being able to boil an egg, or open a bottle of beer with a spoon. But the process of getting there is unbearable. It's like trying to wrestle a pack of wild animals in a small sauna, while they shout "BOOBIES BOOBIES BOOBIES" at the top of their voices. And that's before they're even in the pool.

Things were different when I was growing up in Australia. I don't remember learning to swim – it was something I just knew how to do, like speaking with an upward inflection, and barbecuing. I would toddle off on my bike, wearing only my togs and sandals, a towel dangling over the handlebars. I went swimming in deep bodies of water, jumping off diving boards and swinging off ropes. I was carefree. And I only nearly drowned a few times.

So I looked forward to taking my sweet baby to the pool, envisioning us giggling and smiling as we splashed about. What I didn't realise was that I was about to enter a new circle of hell. Which I suspect operates at about the same temperature as the changing rooms in British swimming pools. Why do they do this? It makes you sweat, causes stress and encourages boiling rage. Especially when the carefully packed swimming bag is emptied into the puddle on the floor. My son likes to add to the chaos by doing a pee, usually such a big one that I can only assume he's been saving it up all week, just for this moment.

Changing rooms induce verbal diarrhoea in my children, who love to loudly describe the scene before them. My favourite quotes have included:

"MUMMY HAS BIG FLOPPY BREASTICLES!"

"Your tummy is HUGE, Mummy. Do you have another baby in there?"

"Why is your front bottom so hairy?"

Once that's over you have to run the gauntlet to the pool, watching out for slippery surfaces, finger-jamming locker doors, and the random biohazards other swimmers have kindly left on the floor. Things my children have tried to put in their mouths include: an old lollipop, a used plaster, a (human?) hairball, a mouldy swimming cap and a wellington boot (not ours).

Then it's time to jump in the water and begin the lesson. Or, if you're my children, sit on the side of the pool refusing to go in for ten minutes, then ignore the teacher completely while dicking about with an old verruca sock you found stuck in the filter.

Afterwards everyone gets to do the first bit all over again, in reverse, while wet, tired, hungry and cold. This is extra fun in winter, when you get the added challenge of having to dry hair while finding missing gloves.

Let's be honest: the best bit about swimming lessons is getting home. There's a huge sense of achievement in knowing your children are one step closer to being less likely to drown. Plus you get to reward yourself for having made sure they got some healthy exercise by downing half a bottle of Chardonnay.

And it's not forever; I know they WILL learn to swim, eventually. I just wish the process of my kids learning a survival skill didn't nearly kill me.

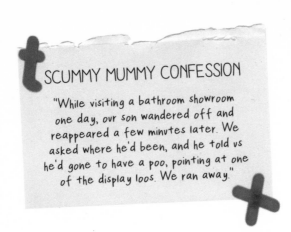

HOW TO DO TOILET TRAINING WITHOUT GOING POTTY

Getting your kid out of nappies is one of the hardest and, frankly, most disgusting jobs you have to do as a parent. Most of us can expect to go through thousands of baby wipes, hundreds of pants, and gallons of gin during the process.

Potty training is so tricky that there are entire books devoted to it. Most of them claim that to succeed you must give your children rewards (bribes) and tell them they are doing a good job (lie). In reality, all the chocolate buttons and promises of trips to Toys 'R' Us in the world won't stop your little darling from saving up a week's worth of poo to decorate Granny's new carpet.

Why should the kids get all the treats, anyway? We're the ones having to endlessly clean all the clothes, sheets, soft furnishings and bottoms. So here's a potty training reward chart for mums and dads.

Potty Training Parenting Goal	Reward
Get through the day without saying "Do you need a wee-wee?" more than a hundred times	1 glass of wine
Look sincere while thanking the nursery staff for returning soiled pants, as if you're going to take them home and bleach them, when actually they're going straight in the bin	Half a bottle
Clean the potty within four hours of use	Gin and tonic
Accidently ask a work client, "Do you need a poo?" because they look a bit fidgety	Shot of tequila
Convince a colleague the stain on your trousers is actually chocolate	Pint of Prosecco
Get your child to do a wee in the park without peeing on their own shoes	Box of house white
Successfully pee in a nappy yourself while caught short in a car park	A magnum of Champagne
Find a mummified poo in the toy box	A case of Scotch

SCUMMY MUMMY CONFESSION

"My 15-year-old daughter brought her new boyfriend home to meet us. I leaned across the worktop and sang, 'Don't you wish your girlfriend was hot like me?' at him. Apparently I'm horrible."

FROM NITS TO NAPPY RASH: SURVIVING THE CALPOL YEARS

All children get ill at some point. In fact, most children get ill all the bloody time. Runny noses, sore throats, chickenpox, tonsillitis, irritating coughs that are magically cured by a healthy dose of Haribo… Then there are infestations to deal with, like nits and worms, not to mention those endless bumps, bruises and mystery rashes.

Basically, becoming a mum means becoming a nurse, doctor, pharmacist, pest control specialist and biohazard disposal expert. You might as well go through your bathroom cabinet and chuck out all those luxury face washes and massage oils; you'll need the room for plasters and antiseptic cream. Don't forget to dedicate an entire shelf or two to Calpol – you cannot own too much. In fact, the smart parent will take out shares in the company and buy a stakehold in Sudocrem while they're at it.

There's no point trying to avoid all this. You can't keep your child in a bubble (we Googled it and it's actually illegal). Birthday parties and play dates are breeding grounds for germs. As for soft play centres… you might as well let your child play in a bin.

SCUMMY MUMMY CONFESSION

"My children call lice their pets."

Sure, you could always be that mum who quietly follows their child around with hand sanitiser and antiseptic wipes, but the germs will

always find a way, and people might get the idea you're just a tiny little bit uptight.

Things were different back in the seventies. Calpol was basically 80% chloroform. Parents thought nothing of letting the dog lick the kids' faces clean, and considered soil one of your five-a-day. (Actually, five-a-day didn't officially exist back then, but it would have been something like: soil, blancmange, Smash, cubes of cheese and pineapple on cocktail sticks, second-hand smoke.)

Today our attitudes to health are different, thankfully. But some things never change: kids will always get poorly, and we'll always need to mop the brow, dole out the medicine and clear up the sick. The reality is that childhood illness is part of your life now, along with disinfectant and rubber sheets.

SCUMMY MUMMY CONFESSION

"When our son was 18 months old, he drank an entire bottle of bubble bath. Accident & Emergency said not to shake him. He burped bubbles for two days."

HOW TO HAVE NITS WITHOUT GOING NUTS

It usually starts with the letter home, written in that passive-aggressive style schools do so well: "We've had some unwelcome visitors in the class..."

As everyone knows, this is code for: "Your grubby child has given everyone the hair plague. Don't come back until you've painted a red cross on your door and shaved his head."

If you've yet to experience the horror of headlice, you might be deluded enough to think it'll never happen to you. But rest assured, one day your kids WILL bring nits home from school, along with the usual collection of weird paintings, shit pottery and letters about not parking by the gates.

It's infuriating that despite the fact that science has brought us space travel and Skype, there's no easy way to get rid of nits. The only option is to comb the buggers out, a painful task for everyone involved. Oh, the whining, the wriggling, the moaning – and then once your husband's done, there are the kids to deal with.

Worst of all, having nits is still taboo in some circles, despite it being such a common parenting experience. Discussing it involves lots of whispering and nervous laughter. It's all about trying to sound jolly while saying things like "Apparently, lice only like really clean hair" as if the particular species of nit on your kid's head only wears White Company cardigans and eats organic.

Basically, nits are no fun. But they are inevitable, so be prepared by creating an Emergency Nit Kit.

Make sure you have these things in stock at all times. If your child is starting school in September, get them now. Seriously. They're more important than the uniform, a coat, shoes, etc.

Another good idea is to make the whole thing a game. Draw up a chart to show which member of the family has the most live nits. We once counted 13 on one comb, and we all cheered.

And remember, you're not alone. Everyone who has children will get nits at some point – probably more than once. It's OK to indulge in a bit of schadenfreude as you picture Wills and Kate combing insects out of each other's hair. (All right, so Wills and Kate probably have a dedicated Nit Butler for this kind of thing, but you get the general idea.)

We'll never win the war on nits, so we might as well chuckle through it. Good luck, everyone!

Emergency Nit Kit

☐ A giant bottle of nit killer, combs and conditioner

☐ Lollipops and kids' DVDs, to distract them from wriggling

☐ Wine, beer and gin, to distract yourself from the whole thing

TRUE STORIES: ELLIE

I once met a doctor at a drinks party. "So what's it like being a GP?" I said.

"I see a lot of well children," she replied. I looked at the floor, thinking of all the times I've taken one of my sons to the surgery because of a minor illness, miniscule injury, or just because he's looking at me a bit funny.

To be fair, many of these appointments have been prompted by my husband, who tends to overreact to signs of illness in his children even more than in himself. (We are talking about a man who, having contracted food poisoning, lay on the bed in his air-conditioned hotel room, watching Wimbledon, and announced: "This is worse than Guantanamo.")

With our eldest, the big issue was speech. By the age of two he had yet to start talking, and we were worried. The health visitor asked if I played music a lot at home. "No," I said smugly. "We always have Radio 4 on." She suggested this was worse, as it meant my poor baby couldn't get a word in edgeways. I was horrified, and terrified his first words would be "North Utsire".

The next time we were at the GP's, for a nasal flu vaccination, I mentioned my concerns to the doctor. Because they're always happy to discuss worries about speech problems while shoving a plastic tube up the nostril of a two-year-old who is trying to kick them in the balls. "I'm sure it'll be fine. OW," he said.

A few months later there was still no change, so I made another appointment to see the same GP. As I opened the door, my son took one look at the guy and shouted: "DON'T STICK ANYTHING UP MY NOSE."

"Your son does not have a speech problem," said the doctor, as we turned and walked away.

Sure enough, within a few weeks, my son was talking non-stop. Not only that, he was using sentences like: "Technically, Mother, that's a spanner, not a wrench."

I've been a bit more relaxed with my second son, as is so often the way of things. But we do still make the odd pointless trip to the GP for some kindly reassurance. I'm so grateful for the opportunity to do that, because we live in a country where healthcare is free.

SCUMMY MUMMY CONFESSION

"I'm a doctor. My son's mum is a paediatric nurse. But Zac was still at the doctor's surgery this morning, with a slightly puffy eye, because WE WANTED IT SEEN TO. I'm more than happy to annoy my doctor constantly, just like most parents."

RED BOOK: THE SCUMMY MUMMIES VERSION

Every parent in Britain is familiar with the Red Book. It's what the health visitor gives you when you have a baby. It's great for making sure you're worrying about all the things you need to worry about, and keeping track of all the things you're doing wrong.

But when it comes to being a Scummy Mummy, the Red Book seems to be missing a few pages. For example, it would be useful to know what you can expect from life as a parent, as shown in this handy graph:

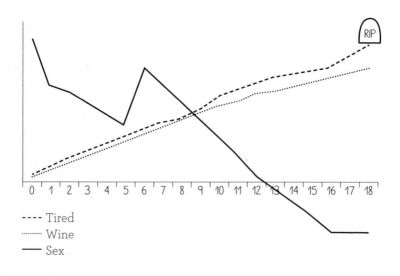

---- Tired
.... Wine
——— Sex

As you can see, the age of the child from 0 to 18 years is shown on the bottom of the graph. The lines indicate the following:

- ---- How tired you're going to be, until you end up dead
- .... How much wine you'll be drinking
- ——— How much sex you'll be having
  (note the peak for the conception of the second child)

The Red Book also has lots of pages where you can log your child's firsts – smile, word and so on. But wouldn't it be great if you could record those scummy moments as well? For instance:

FIRST PUBLIC PELVIC FLOOR DISASTER

Got pissed at a children's birthday party and decided to have a go on the trampoline. Never again.

FIRST SWEAR WORD

"Fuck." Said in the middle of her cousin's Christening.

MOST IMPRESSIVE PROJECTILE WEE

At the baby-weighing clinic. Pissed directly into the Health Visitor's face.

FIRST POO UP ENTIRE BACK

Middle of the Tate Modern on a busy Sunday afternoon. We had to cut off her clothes.

BIGGEST TANTRUM

In the middle of a DIY shop, because I wouldn't let him eat compost.

FIRST INAPPROPRIATE QUESTION

Eldest asked Aunty Faye why she has a beard.

When you're new to parenting, the Red Book can seem like a massive deal. But like nappies, *Tree Fu Tom* and not owning any jeans that aren't held together with dirt and snot, it won't always be such a big part of your life.

Years from now, you'll wistfully flick through the pages, being reminded of all those happy trips to the vaccination clinic, and the time you nearly had a breakdown because her weight dropped from the 78th to the 77th percentile. Then you can chuck it in the bin.

TRUE STORIES: HELEN

For me, looking after sick children has been one of the hardest experiences of parenthood. I really struggle with seeing my babies in distress, the sleepless nights, and scrubbing sick out of the carpet. But I can just about cope with illness when it's in my own home. Having to deal with it on a 24-hour flight to Australia is a different story – a much smellier, shittier story.

Even if everyone's in perfect health, long-haul flights with kids are a nightmare. Who wants to spend an entire night and day in the sky with a toddler who only wants to run down the aisles and swing off the luggage locker handles while throwing raisins in people's faces? Fucking nobody, that's who.

But just to make things extra exciting, my kids like to save up their illnesses all year for when we're airborne. For example, I'll never forget the time my ten-month-old baby started sprouting chickenpox blisters somewhere over Rajasthan.

I desperately tried to breastfeed him through it. The poor air steward didn't know where to look as I attempted to shove both boobs in my baby's mouth like fleshy burritos – but he wasn't having any of it. Eventually we broke all the rules and fed him ice cream for the rest of the flight. When you're stuck in the sky, the last thing you're worried about is whether they're getting their five-a-day. You just have to get through it alive, or if things are really bad, pray for a crash.

Our next flightmare occurred a year later, pretty much to the day. My eldest child began throwing up seven minutes after we got in the taxi to Heathrow. Within ten minutes, we were all covered in sick. We made an emergency stop at a Pret A Manger in central London. I dumped all our clothes in the sanitary bin, put everyone in pyjamas, and rushed out before anyone could tell us off for not buying a croissant. A quick wipe down of the taxi with half a packet of baby wipes and a new M&S coat, and we were on the road again.

Unfortunately, the vomiting did not stop until we reached Tullamarine Airport 24 hours later. The flight was a blur of sick bags and endless apologies. We survived with the help of *My Little Pony* on repeat and a medicinal Singapore Sling for me.

But my personal favourite was the time we realised we had head lice just north of Kuala Lumpur. There we were – me, the husband, the six-year-old and the toddler – all scratching our filthy, infested hair like a bunch of feral gorillas. And just to make sure everyone knew what was happening, the kids kept shouting: "My head's itchy, Mummy! It's REALLY itchy!"

Who knows what mysterious illness we will contract the next time we fly? All I know is we'll all be wearing plastic ponchos and shaving our heads.

FANTASY VS REALITY: ILLNESSES

If you're worried your child is ill, the best thing to do is visit your doctor, health visitor, or hospital. Probably best to stay away from Dr Google, as this handy table illustrates.

Symptom	Illness, as diagnosed by Google	Doctor's diagnosis
Runny nose	Pneumonia	Leave it for a bit; come back in a few days if it's still happening
Sore throat	Bubonic plague	Leave it for a bit; come back in a few days if it's still happening
Cough	Tuberculosis	Seriously, he's not a Brontë
Vivid red rash over entire face	Scarlet fever	Don't let her play with marker pens
Farts all the time	Irritable bowel syndrome	He is a small boy
Verruca	Invasion by mysterious foot-dwelling tapeworm that only exists in Malawian lakes	Get out

ACTUAL TOP TIP

Jessie McCulloch, health visitor and children's nurse

"Health visitors (HVs) are there to provide support. Some people think you have to make a huge effort before we come round, but I expect to see new parents in their PJs, and we really don't care if you haven't washed up last night's dinner.

"It might feel weird inviting a stranger into your home to talk about the highs and lows of parenthood. But your HV is trained to help with any practical, emotional and financial challenges you might be facing. We're used to panicked phone calls about the fact your baby's poo has suddenly turned green. No question is too silly!

"Never worry about 'bothering' your HV. We can always make time for families who need extra support, or find the best person to help. Being honest about your feelings really makes a difference. Telling someone you are feeling low can be difficult, but you could call, write a note, or ask to talk in private if it's a busy clinic.

"HVs can help with everything from coping with post-natal depression and illness to finding childcare and getting rid of nits. We love helping parents find their confidence, and working with families is an absolute privilege."

SCUMMY MUMMY CONFESSION

"A year after I stopped breastfeeding, I said to my doctor, 'I still produce milk when I squeeze my nipples.' He bluntly replied, 'Stop squeezing your nipples.'"

TIGERS VS HELICOPTERS: WHAT'S YOUR PARENTING STYLE?

According to the old saying, babies don't come with a manual. But that's not strictly true. Sure, there's no pamphlet that plops out with the placenta, but there are about a million handbooks about how to raise kids. The problem is they all say different things.

Should you use the naughty step or time-outs? Hire a nanny or find a nursery? Co-sleep or let them cry it out? Don't ask us; we haven't got a fucking clue.

Go ahead, read those books if you want to – you may well find some useful info that suits your own parenting style. But if you're expecting to discover the secret to being a perfect parent every second of every day, you might as well flick through an Argos catalogue. It's just as likely to contain all the answers, and at least they have some really good deals on handheld blenders.

The thing is, every parent-child relationship is different, and families come in all sorts of shapes, sizes and configurations. Everyone has a unique experience and perspective. So no wonder there isn't a one-size-fits-all solution, and most mums and dads will tell you they're making it up as they go along.

Having said all that, parents do have lots in common. We all love our children, and we're trying to do the best we can with the resources we have available. We could sit around reading parenting books and arguing about attachment theory all day, but at some point we're all going to end up with shit on our hands.

Let's be honest, we've all been in situations where we've judged other parents. That's because a) we're secretly looking for reassurance about our own failings, and b) we're human. The trick is to remember that none of us is perfect; everyone has had shouty days, disastrous bedtimes and sleepless nights over whether we're doing it all wrong. We should help each other out instead of judging, at least in public.

SCUMMY MUMMY CONFESSION

"I was sick in the bins outside Church Twin Club. I was just hungover, but I pretended it was a nervous breakdown."

TRUE STORIES: ELLIE

Before I had kids, I didn't even really realise there is such a thing as different parenting styles. I just assumed everyone sort of followed the same rules – be kind but firm, try not to shout, don't let them eat Mars Bars for breakfast, etc. I remember thinking: "How hard can it be?" HAHAHAHAHAHAHAHA.

The books are no help. The first one I read was *The Baby Whisperer*, which is all about following the E.A.S.Y. routine. It might work for some people, but all my attempts to stick to the plan resulted in Exasperation, Aggravation, Swearing and Yelling. I ended up taking the whole thing literally, whispering, "Go to sleep, please go to sleep, pleeeease" in my baby's ear for hours on end.

Then there was *The No-Cry Sleep Solution*. I did all the things – kept the sleep diary, did the Pantley pull-off, tried the gradual retreat. None of it worked. Instead I invented my own method, the 'No Sleep, Just Have a Cry Solution', where you give up and have a good old whinge. You're still knackered, but at least you don't have to spend four hours patting anyone.

Eventually I realised there was a fundamental problem with these books – my baby hadn't read them. How was he supposed to know that eating comes first, followed by an activity, after which you roll over and pass out for six hours straight? He had clearly been reading a different book, perhaps one titled *Party On, Boob: Why Sleeping for More than 45 Minutes Is for Mugs*.

Really, the best advice I got was from all the other parents who said: "It's not forever." That's hard to believe sometimes, but of course it is true – eventually all babies WILL sleep through the night, use the potty, and understand that forks are not for poking out eyes.

However, it's also true that old problems get replaced by new ones. Now my eldest can not only walk and talk, but call me a massive idiot and run away. He argues like a lawyer and has an astonishingly good memory for detail… "But Mummy, you PROMISED I could have a purple Fruit Shoot that time I let George have a sip of mine while we were waiting to go to the Tiny Truckers ride at Chessington World of Adventures on 19th July 2013."

Now I skip the parenting books and go straight to other mums and dads for words of wisdom. "Follow your instincts" seems to be a common theme. But sometimes my instinct is to shout, or throw the bloody water pistol in the bin, or run out of the front door and keep on running until I reach Dundee, where I will set up a tea shop called Mrs McQuiet's that is only for calm people with no children.

Then there's "Be consistent." But this is not always easy to do when dealing with small children who are anything but. They will declare ham is their favourite food for two years, then one day – perhaps because they feel like it, perhaps because they somehow know there's nothing else in the fridge – they will react to a piece of ham being placed on their plate as if someone has just presented them with a dead pigeon, garnished with dirt and finished with a cat's-piss *jus*.

But while there's more to parenting styles than I thought, my own way of doing things isn't actually that far away from those old ideals. I try to be kind, and to at least look like I'm being firm, even when I feel wobbly. I do my best not to shout, and when I'm terrible at this, I just start again the next day. And I don't let them eat Mars Bars for breakfast unless it's Easter.

Most of the time I have no idea what I'm doing. From talking to other mums, though, I'm not sure anyone does. So I just carry on, trying to do my best, and hoping that, with a little bit of luck, it's good enough.

MEET THE EXPERTS

With so many books out there offering advice, it can be difficult to know what the right parenting style is for you. So we asked two leading experts to give us their take on some of the big dilemmas.

First up is Australian-born Judith Krank, author of the best-selling books *Birthing in Thongs* and *No Worries, Mate: How to Bring Up Bonza Kids*.

"Anyone who's chucked a child out their yoni knows it's a big bloody deal," says Judith.

"All my principles of parenting have been inspired by the beautiful raw energy of the Australian bush, the traditional practices of our indigenous peoples, and Helen Daniels off *Neighbours*."

Judith has raised her two children, Dixie-Doo and Crush, according to her own version of attachment theory. "I call it Barnacle Parenting," she explains. "Being a helicopter mum is no good – if you're hovering about, you might slice off their limbs. Best to keep them physically attached to you at all times, like a limpet, or a wart."

Offering a different perspective is Margot Chesney-Hooter. She became the UK's leading authority on firm but fair parenting with the 1974 publication of *Come On Now: How to Raise Children Who Can Look after Themselves*.

"When I gave birth on the coffee farm in Kenya, there was no such thing as parenting," says Margot. "You had the baby, you sewed yourself up, and you got on with things."

As the saying goes, it takes a village to raise a child ("which is why I mainly employed the locals to look after mine"), but Margot believes kids need only three things to be happy: "fresh air, independence and sticks." Her own children, of which she has "three or four", were "never happier than when romping around outdoors, building dens, and stamping on the heads of venomous snakes".

According to Margot, there's too much fuss about raising kids these days. To paraphrase Germaine Greer, she thinks children come up just the same, brought up or not. "I'm no feminist, though," she is keen to point out. "You say men and women are equal – I say, show me a man who can pull a Land Rover out of a ditch with a girdle."

Judith and Margot have quite different opinions about parenting. Here's a table so you can work out which approach suits you.

Dilemma	Judith says	Margot says
"Should I give my baby a dummy?"	Every parent must make the choice that's right for them – but remember, dummies can be hard to give up, like cocaine. Try seeking out natural alternatives, like a piece of sugar cane.	Nothing wrong with dummies – my cousin Binky has one, and he's 47. They're ideal for keeping kids quiet, or in Binky's case, limiting the racism expounded on social occasions.
"My son's just covered the entire kitchen wall in green felt tip. What should I do?"	Celebrate! Praise your child's bold creative talents and see this as an opportunity to collaborate with him. Why not grab your découpage kit and turn it into a family mural?	Give him a bucket of turps and a sponge, and tell him that by suppertime you want that wall gleaming like the Taj at sundown.
"My daughter hates wearing shoes. How do I get her to keep them on?"	People have been going barefoot for literally millennia, and it's a great way to make a physical connection with nature. Just watch out for broken glass and dog excrement.	Do up the laces with a double sheepshank and a midshipman's hitch.

"How much screen time should my child have each day?"	Children are digital natives, but it's important we curate their cultural experience. So you should only let them watch BBC documentaries.	All children who watch television turn into square-eyed homicidal maniacs. They're better off learning to read and play canasta.
"How do I get my baby to sleep through the night?"	Try allowing the baby to sleep in your bed, or better still, on your face.	Rum.

SCUMMY MUMMY CONFESSION

"As we drove past the local pub one day, my daughter exclaimed, 'Oh look! That's the café Grandma takes me to!' All pubs are now referred to as 'cafés'."

SCUMMY MUMMY CONFESSION

"We went on holiday with both sets of grandparents. I complained to my mum that my husband's parents don't pay for anything. The next time we discussed going for dinner, my seven-year-old son said: 'Gramps, Mummy said that next time you need to pay. So tonight, YOU PAY.'"

SCUMMY MUMMY CONFESSION

"My mum asked my son what he does at school. He said: 'Nothing. I just play all day, and then I go home and have a bottle of wine.'"

TRUE STORIES: HELEN

When I had my first child, I gave birth not only to a baby, but to a whole new set of relationships. I was now the mother of someone's precious grandchild. With this new role came great expectations, boundless love and one or two teeny-tiny clashes of opinion about parenting choices.

I knew from the start that my mothering style would be different to my own mum's. As the daughter of a vicar, I spent my early years in a haze of hymns and casserole-fuelled Bible studies classes. Basically, I grew up in the Aussie version of *The Vicar of Dibley*.

My mum is not a Scummy Mummy. She is neat, calm, hardly drinks wine, always wears aprons and never swears. I am more relaxed and casual in my approach to parenting (lazy). My kitchen table is more likely to be covered in Lego and pizza crusts than lace doilies and freshly polished silver.

I never planned to bring up my kids so far from home. When I left Australia at the age of 27, I figured I'd be back in a few years, ready to settle down. But I ended up giving birth in the UK, and then found I was too tired to contemplate walking to Asda, let alone catch a plane to Australia.

Bringing up kids without family nearby has been tough. What I wouldn't have given in those early years for a relative who could take the baby off my hands just for an hour, so I could wash my hair or drink a coffee. But there are advantages to the distance – communicating via Skype means I can strategically avoid showing my mother-in-law the piles of unwashed dishes and unironed clothes, and I don't have to worry about her accidentally sitting on some old Plasticine, or worse.

Another bonus is that we get to have fantastic holidays where everyone is on their BEST BEHAVIOUR. Having a limited time together motivates you to be jolly and tolerant, mostly. And it's a great opportunity for grannies to see what life is *really* like outside those filtered iPhone photos.

Of course, that doesn't stop them chipping in with some helpful 'feedback'. Here are some of my favourite comments from visiting grannies:

Scanning my messy lounge: "Oh Helen, it's wonderful that you're such a... *relaxed* mother."

Watching my daughter go off to a birthday party: "Hmm. That's a lovely dress, dear. Do you want me to iron it for you?"

Seeing my son's hair for the first time in a year: "Darling, do you own a hairbrush?"

And the classic: "Have ever thought about feeding them fruit?"

Thinking about these moments makes me laugh, now, but at the time I felt a bit wounded. Having done most of my parenting without help, I would congratulate myself just for getting through the day with everyone still alive. So every comment felt like a criticism, and every suggestion seemed like an insult.

But now a bit of time has passed and I've had a lot more sleep, I can see the grandparents meant well. We were all just trying to work out how to perform these new roles.

Sharing the same DNA doesn't mean you share the same ideas about ironing, bedtime and hairbrushing. But one thing we do have in common is that we want our kids to be happy and safe. And if I get to be a granny, I expect I'll have a hard time keeping some things to myself, too...

TRUE STORIES: DIFFERENT PERSPECTIVES

Just as there's a wide range of parenting styles, there are lots of different domestic set-ups. Here a stay-at-home dad, a single mum and an adoptive mum discuss their experiences of parenthood.

Stay-at-home dad Steve Hill writes:
According to recent data, an estimated one in seven full-time parents is male. We're a silent minority, stalking the nation's playgrounds as horrified mothers keep their offspring close.

It's not that bad, really, although the early years are a struggle, with almost every conversation involving either leakage or tearing. Fair enough. The mothers have each squeezed a human out of trap one, whereas all I've done is chuck my muck, an ostensibly daily occurrence-turned-life-changing event.

Once the kids start school, it's more of a level playing field. I now consider myself integrated to the point where my arrival at the gates isn't automatically greeted with revulsion. In fact, some of the other parents seem actively pleased to see me.

I have even been entrusted with hosting play dates. I was initially wary of this myself, displaying a kind of inverted sexism, as if having a cock and balls somehow precludes one from putting a supermarket pizza in front of a kid before locking him in the garden.

Despite being the only dad in the park after school, I don't feel emasculated. In fact, it's almost the opposite: the male of the pack assigned heavy lifting and vigorous swing pushing. Now that they've ascertained that I'm not a child-catcher, the mothers entrust me to look after their kids, hold their babies and even share heartbreaking tales of absent fathers.

The dads that occasionally show up seem to silently resent the amount of time I spend with their wives, some of whom are slightly in love with me, naturally – they are only human, after all: mere flesh and blood.

Talking of which, when the chat turns back to pregnancy and childbirth, the headphones go in, as there's always a crucial cricket match I have to listen to, even when there isn't.

As for the child, he is of course an unrepentant sociopath with a genital obsession. On the plus side, he's very good at darts, video games and swearing.

Single mum Alison Sakai writes:
The weirdest bit was probably being a single pregnant person. Every time the pregnancy app suggested to 'put your feet up and get your partner to do the cooking', I nearly smashed the iPhone to bits. I vowed to write a pregnancy book that removed all references to partners. (Obviously, I couldn't be arsed to actually do this.)

Looking back, the first year was really difficult. It was lonely and tiring and boring. When you're on your own, there's no evening homecoming to look forward to – no respite, no grown-up chat, no one to share those tiny milestones with. If I didn't leave the house I'd suddenly realise I hadn't spoken out loud all day, and panic that my baby would grow up mute. (She never shuts up now.)

Mum friends are vital for providing practical support and keeping your sanity intact, but they don't always remember your situation is a bit different. I sympathised when my mates complained about how little their husbands did to help, and silently wondered whether it was better or worse to have no help at all.

Now she's a bit older, Milly stays at her dad's a couple of nights a week, and this works brilliantly for everyone. She loves spending time with him, and I get proper nights out where I don't have to rush home for the babysitter. I'm pretty sure getting regular time to myself makes me a better parent when I am on duty.

Being a single parent is really common these days, but occasionally you get reminded that it's not so long since there was a real stigma to it. One old guy I spoke to tutted at me, saying: "It's not really fair on the child though, is it?" I was too apoplectic with rage to respond.

Milly has a stable family life – it's just split over more locations. For her, this is normality. A few months after she started school, she came home and announced in astonishment: "Mummy, some of the children at school have only got one house!" She thinks the kids in nuclear families are a bit deprived.

It's now five years since I had her and on balance, I think I'm better as a single parent than I would be as a 'not single' parent. Her dad and I try to co-parent in a consistent, positive way, and it's working well for both of us. And it looks like Milly is turning out OK, too.

Adoptive mum Carolyn Robertson writes:
I am an adoptive gay mum to two boys. Life as an adopter is a never-ending rollercoaster of amazing highs, and reach-for-the-gin lows. Seeing our boys grow and flourish is the most rewarding experience. But there's also a lot of frustration as we deal with extreme and challenging behaviours, and have to fight like mad to get support.

When we first became parents I thought being gay would be the common denominator, and that I'd find kindred spirits in other lezza mums. Actually, the big bonding factor has been adoption, and we mainly hang out with gay and straight adopters.

Being an adoptive parent presents many challenges and is very different to having birth children. Now that single parenthood is more socially acceptable, most adopted children have not been relinquished; almost all have been removed from their original birth family. The vast majority have experienced trauma and loss, and many have suffered abuse.

Our first son came to us at eight months old. We were incredibly lucky to adopt a baby, and loved getting to share so many firsts (teeth! steps! words!).

Our second son came from a different family, just before he turned two. He had a trickier start in life, and has put us through our paces. We have had to take up a lot of professional help to support him, and there have been some tough times at both home and school.

We love our boys with a deep, fierce passion, but we recognise that they are more vulnerable than children from birth families. They struggle with self-esteem and identity issues and occasionally stupid comments from other adults: "Are they real brothers?" "They're so lucky to have you..." The worst is when we're on our knees, struggling with difficult behaviours, and someone says: "Oh, it's just boy stuff, lots of kids do that..." This makes me want to scream, if I'm honest.

Some days I completely forget our sons are adopted; other days, it feels very apparent. We are open with them about their adoption and we regularly send and receive letters from their birth families. Initially this contact freaked me out, but now I believe it is really healthy for everyone. Our boys will always be part of another family. We embrace this, and I think an open approach has given them more stability and understanding about their life journey.

Despite the tough times, I absolutely love being an adoptive mum. I am extremely proud of our family.

SCUMMY MUMMY CONFESSION

"My son has developed the habit of weeing in glasses during an emergency. One day Grandad drank his wee, thinking it was Foster's."

WORKING 5 TO 9: BALANCING BOARD MEETINGS WITH BEDTIME

Juggling motherhood and work can be tough, according to everything written about juggling motherhood and work *ever*. Let's be clear – looking after a child IS a job. There are bonuses, of course; you get to wear the same PJs three days in a row, watch all the *Peppa Pig* you want and eat a lot of crusts. But it's also a lot of hard work, with no holiday, no sick leave and a boss who bites your nipples.

So being a working mum involves having two careers. It's a daily struggle to stay calm in the face of tantrums, fighting, generally unreasonable behaviour and no one ever flushing the toilet – and then you have to deal with it all again when you get home.

The good news is that being a parent can have real advantages in the workplace. It all starts with maternity leave. This is an ideal time to develop your professional skills and appreciate your own talents. If you thought you were good multi-tasking before you had kids, just wait till you have to combine board meetings and spreadsheets with nappy changing and nits.

You will impress yourself with your ability to answer 55 emails while expressing milk.

SCUMMY MUMMY
CONFESSION

"I regularly go to work knowing there's sick on my shoulder."

You will give yourself a pat on the back for remembering to source that Gruffalo costume for World Book Day, even though you only had three hours of broken sleep. You will high-five yourself for wiping a toddler's bottom while simultaneously breastfeeding his sister, ringing the plumber and explaining why dogs can't talk. Or you would if you had a free hand.

As with so many aspects of parenting, the secret to success (or at least not going bananas) involves doing some planning, obeying your gut instinct and winging it a bit. Trust yourself to make the decisions that work for your family and ignore the unwarranted opinions you'll inevitably receive from your relatives, your boss, the lady behind you in the queue at the post office, etc. If you can't ignore them, just smile and nod patiently while internally telling them to shove it up their arse. Trust us, it works.

SCUMMY MUMMY CONFESSION

"Child: 'Is Daddy going to work today?'
Me: 'Yes he is.'
Child: 'Oh for fuck's sake, Rob.'"

HOW TO BE A GREAT WORKING MUM

Motherhood is great for learning extra skills, from how to change a nappy in the dark to the best way of getting mashed banana out of a cat's ears. Here's how to make the most of those newfound abilities at work.

Skill 1: Prioritising
Before you had kids, your morning routine probably involved achieving the perfect blow-dry and flawless make-up – but try doing that while persuading a toddler to eat his breakfast instead of the remote control.

Being a mum makes you a whizz at saving time by focusing on what's important. It's easier to hide that unwashed hair under a hat, such as a stylish beret. Or solve two problems at once with a sombrero – it will balance out those dark circles, so there's no need for all that Touche Éclat.

Skill 2: Presentation
Parenting provides the perfect opportunity to overhaul your personal style by exploring the world of accessories. Brooches, scarves and giant necklaces are great for covering snot stains. They also act as a distraction, drawing your colleagues' attention away from the Weetabix stuck to your bottom.

Skill 3: Time-saving
Now you're a parent you don't have time to waste, but you do have ways to move things along. If you ever need to bring a boring work conversation to an end, just start showing the person pictures of your kids. You can also shut down meetings pretty quickly by talking about your suspected prolapse.

Skill 4: Forward Planning
As a parent, you learn to be a master of scheduling. It's not just meetings and conference calls – you're also keeping track of ballet lessons and school plays, while factoring in time to do the supermarket shop and fight with your partner.

Show off about how busy you are by buying an expensive, leather-bound family planner with 28 individually tabbed sections.

It will make you look super-organised and competent (until you lose it, the dog eats it, or the kids set fire to it).

Skill 5: Asset Management
People without kids often just see coffee as a drink. The rest of us understand that it is the elixir of life.

As a working mum, you will develop an encyclopaedic knowledge of every coffee chain within 500 metres of the office. You will know exactly how many Nespresso pods are in the office kitchen at any moment. Your colleagues will ensure the stock is regularly topped up, because no one wants a repeat of the day you were found weeping under the sink, threatening to punch everyone in the face.

Skill 6: People Management
If a workmate is disagreeing with you, use the same voice you use on your kids to explain calmly but authoritatively why they're talking shit. Encourage your subordinates to hit deadlines by telling them to get the work done by the time you count to three.

Putting colleagues on the naughty step is probably taking it too far, but there's nothing wrong with rewarding a job well done with a WOW card and a packet of chocolate buttons.

Skill 7: Team-building
Now you're going straight home after work to see the kids, you can feel smug every morning when your workmates turn up hungover, complaining about how that cheeky pint turned into an all-nighter. They don't know you sank an entire bottle of Sauvignon Blanc between bedtime and passing out on the sofa at 9.30PM.

Save up all your after-work alcohol units for those big occasions. There's nothing like spending the work Christmas party telling your colleagues what's wrong with your marriage, or informing the keynote speaker at that important conference that you haven't had sex for six months.

In Conclusion
Being a parent doesn't mean you have to stop climbing the career ladder. It just means you need to pack some baby wipes to clean the porridge off the rungs.

ACTUAL TOP TIP

Shannon-Kate Archer, employment lawyer

"Communication and organisation are critical to any successful return to work. Contact your employer a reasonable amount of time before you go back. Ask what work you'll be doing, explain your childcare arrangements, and if you need flexibility, request it early on.

"Organisation means putting your name down for every childcare provider in the country, and getting used to being told the waiting list is longer than the Domesday Book. Stay in touch with your first-choice provider (but try not to stalk them).

"You'll need new clothes. Try to avoid buttons and shoelaces, at least for the first year. They take too long. One-pieces are good. Don't get dressed till you've served the kids breakfast. And remember, baby wipes are a lot cheaper than dry cleaning."

ACTUAL TOP TIP

Inga Lyon, nanny

"I know it's hard to leave your child with someone else, especially at first. But try to say a quick goodbye and then go – sticking around and letting the baby see you upset just makes it more stressful for everyone. And it's amazing how quickly kids cheer up once their mum is out of sight..."

SCUMMY MUMMY CONFESSION

"On the way to a day out, we stopped at a client's house to drop something off. Our daughter was sick on their drive. By the time we found something to clean up the vomit, their dog had eaten it."

TRUE STORIES: ELLIE

When I was pregnant with my first child, I was convinced there was no way I wouldn't want to go back to work full-time. I loved my job, I was in line for a big promotion and I got to travel all over the world. "What could be better than this?" I thought.

Then I had my baby. Within a week, I'd decided we had to move to the country, where I would spend the rest of my days baking cakes and making bunting. My husband just nodded and smiled, having already learned this is the best way to interact with a woman who's had less than three hours' sleep.

But as the months went by, and the hormones settled down, I realised I hate bunting and I can't bake for shit. I started to feel like the endless cycle of breastfeeding, nappy changing and buggy pushing was making my brain soft around the edges. I was ready to go back to work.

It was hard waving goodbye to my baby that first day. But it took all of about 20 minutes to get over it, that being roughly the time it takes to drink a hot cup of tea in peace. And when my mum returned my son that evening, beaming with joy and all limbs intact, I knew we were going to be alright.

Within a few weeks, I felt confident enough to sign up to spend a whole night away for our annual company conference in Brighton. I was keen to show my colleagues that motherhood hadn't altered my professional commitment, that I was still a strong, capable and essential member of the workforce. I undermined this somewhat by delivering a lengthy speech about how much I appreciated their support, which ended with me bursting into tears. Guess I was still a bit hormonal after all.

That evening, it was time for the traditional post-conference team-building session (massive piss-up). This being my first proper night out in over a year, I obviously got hugely overexcited, drank

800 glasses of wine and sank a load of sambuca shots – something I'd decided I was too old for about seven years previously.

I'm pretty sure the karaoke was my idea, although I can't remember who started beatboxing the *Super Mario Bros.* theme tune first. I do know it was me who suggested we all run down to the sea and go for a paddle at 2AM.

At the time, I felt like a wild, free-spirited creature, demonstrating to all the world that I still knew how to embrace fun and adventure. The next day, when I woke up to ruined heels and a hole in my trousers, covered in blood and seawater, I felt like a dick.

Since then, I've realised the trick with both nights out and work in general is to strike a balance. No one wants to sit in the pub looking at photos of my baby all night, but there's no point in pretending I'm not a mum, either. It's part of my identity now. Combining that with the professional side of myself is hard sometimes, but it is possible. And it's still a lot easier than trying to run down a pebble beach while pissed in stilettos.

SCUMMY MUMMY CONFESSION

"My laundry basket is always overflowing, so sometimes I use a carrier bag for the extra dirty washing. I sent my husband to school with his lunch in a carrier bag, and when he pulled out his sandwiches at his desk, he also produced a pair of my daughter's dirty underwear. He is a secondary-school teacher."

HOW TO BE A MUMPREPRENEUR

Hiya, lovelies!!! Foofy St. Clair here. I'm a very proud mummy to three beautiful dogs, and two kids. I'm also a proud mumprepreneur. *Check out my blog, Cupcakes and Pupcakes! And also my Instagram and Facebook and Twitter and YouTube and Snapchat and WhatsApp.* **#sharingiscaring**

I have dedicated my life to creating the most inspiring photos of small cakes and small dogs on the internet. It all began three years ago when my chihuahua Poofy and I were sharing a red-velvet rum baba in the Harrods food hall. I took a photo for Instagram, and within half an hour I had more than four likes! I knew it was the beginning of a wonderful new career. **#mumspiration**

But actually, I have loved cakes ever since boarding school. The dorm larder was like a second home to me. As Mummy always used to say, cakes are like friends – it's good not to have too many, and if they are too rich, they make you feel sick. Anyway, who needs friends when you've got pastry? **#igetbywithalittlehelpfrommyflans**

Being a blogger has taken me to places I never dreamed of visiting, like Vienna, Prague and Dalston. But although my life looks like one long tea party, it's actually a lot of hard work. I once sprained a finger trying to put a dachshund in a doily ruff. Then there was the time I had a severe allergic reaction to a cronut, not to mention the permanent eye-strain from trying to choose between the Valencia and Chrome filters. **#instagrargh**

If you're thinking of becoming a mumprepreneur, the good news is that literally anyone can do it – I am living proof! All you need is an idea, a camera, some really good lighting, a MacBook Air, editing software and loads and loads of time. But there are some things you need to think about first.

Pick a Project
Make sure your blog focuses on something that's really important to you, like your children, or your Cath Kidston luggage tag collection.

Create Unique Content

You've got to offer your followers something they won't find anywhere else. For example, I make cupcakes inspired by celebrities, like the Gwyneth, which is made from avocado, quinoa and sandpaper, or the Middleton, which is really beautiful and elegant but tastes very bland. My favourite, though, is the Mummy, which is made from gin and tears.

Location, Location, Location

Convert your spare fifth bedroom into a bespoke photography studio, or 'Instaroom'. Make sure everything's white and superglue all your lovely objets down, in case the dogs or children manage to get in.

Keep It 'Real'

People want to see how you really live, for the eight minutes a day you're taking photos for social media. So keep lots of kilim throws around to cover up stains, and bin bags for quickly getting rid of messy toys.

Use Loads of Hashtags

Everything's more interesting when you put a hash in front of it. **#amiright #iknowiam #seriously #canthavetoomany #seewhatimean**

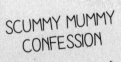

SCUMMY MUMMY
CONFESSION

"I was so hungover from my work Christmas party I couldn't make breakfast for my kids, so as a 'special treat', I gave them mince pies."

TRUE STORIES: HELEN

Returning to work after the birth of my baby made me ask myself some difficult questions. Should I go part-time? What's the best type of childcare? And where the hell do I find workwear that will fit over my giant boobs?

In the end I chose to go back three days a week, found a local nursery and replaced my entire wardrobe with Lycra and capes. None of these decisions were easy.

Going part-time meant we had a lot less money, and I felt I wasn't on top of either my work or my parenting. The endless relay between nursery and the office left me permanently frazzled. I lived on coffee, refined carbs and stress, and my conversations consisted of jumbled words and awkward apologies.

Luckily, I had fantastic support from my working-mum colleagues. They provided me with everything a mother returning to work needs – a sympathetic ear, lots of tea, chocolate Hobnobs, and a lockable toilet. There are few greater pleasures in this world than that first poo at work, in silence, and alone.

However, childcare was a big issue for me. With no family around, nursery seemed like the best option, but I had no idea how to pick the right one. I did all the right things: visiting lots of different places, asking the staff the important questions ("Are you a terrorist?"). It felt like those awkward house-share interviews from my twenties, except without having to worry whether they're into death metal and loud sex.

In the end I just went with my gut instinct. I realised nurseries are like husbands: you have to pick the one you think is right for you, and just sort of hope it works out.

Plus, the nursery I chose was local and affordable. In fact, after paying for childcare, I was left with a whole £50 in wages at the end of the month. Surely this was worth three days a week of work and exhaustion?

But I really struggled with leaving my screaming baby in an unknown place with unknown people. I remember hearing her cry as I walked down the road, and crying myself. I definitely didn't feel like I was 'having it all'.

It wasn't long, though, before things settled down. My little one stopped crying at drop-off and was a happy bunny when I picked her up. I started to enjoy the novelty of being able to finish entire thoughts, sentences and hot drinks. My boobs deflated and I was able to ditch the capes. I felt like a proper grown-up again, and proud of myself for making it work. Then, of course, I got pregnant with number two...

SCUMMY MUMMY
CONFESSION

"Once, I was looking for a pen in my handbag during an important meeting, and I found a dirty nappy."

GAME: SNAKES AND CAREER LADDERS

21	22	Your first paycheck! It all goes to the nursery	You get invited to a conference in Vegas! The kids get chicken-pox	25
20	19	No one notices your shoes don't match!	You spray milk in the IT guy's eye :(Poor Graham	16
START! Return to work!	2	3	You get through a meeting without yawning!	5

26	Your boss finds out you secretly call him Mr Tumble	28	You give everyone nits	IT'S FRIDAY! Drink a whole bottle of wine
15	14	13	12	11
6	7	You go a whole day without mentioning your kids!	You arrive at work on time AND snot free!	10

SCHOOL OF FRAUGHT: DEALING WITH PHONICS, FÊTES AND FRIENDSHIPS

Starting school is a huge milestone. In the run-up to the big day, you're likely find yourself dealing with tears, tantrums and worries about fitting in. Your child might also be upset.

But the trouble starts well before then, with choosing a school. Not that there's always much of a choice. Forget any visions you have of finding the perfect academic haven for your little one, complete with its own organic orchard and symphony orchestra. By the time you've been on a few visits, you'll be grateful to find a school within 17 miles of your house that has chairs and is not on fire.

Or, you may find yourself becoming one of those parents who will do anything to get their child into a particular school. This might mean faking religious beliefs, bribing the headteacher, or sending the local council proof you're in the catchment area by emailing them a photo of the tent you've put up in the playground. ("We regret to inform you that due to an especially high demand for school places this year, the boundary for inclusion only extends to the girls' toilets.")

So just getting your child to school on that first day feels like a huge achievement. You will soon learn, however, that this is only

SCUMMY MUMMY CONFESSION

"On Friday, my son went to school with his pyjamas under his uniform. I just couldn't argue any more."

the beginning – all that jumping through hoops was just training for the gigantic obstacle course of admin and hassle you'll be tackling for the next seven years.

You will not believe the volume of newsletters and forms a single school can generate. Your diary will be filled with fairs, concerts, birthday parties and play dates, not to mention World Book Day, International Week, Yet Another Invented Occasion You Must Make a Cake For, etc.

Good luck if you are not already an Oscar-winning costume designer with a cupboard full of Velcro and felt. Thanks to Pinterest, slashing a hole in a pillow slip just won't cut it any more. And if you can't bake, you'd better learn – or at least make a list of all the petrol stations that sell Victoria sponges and are open past 10PM on a Sunday night.

But it's not all bad. It's great to watch your kids take their first steps into the world, make new friends and perhaps even learn some stuff. Plus, you now have more time to piss about on Facebook and watch *Judge Rinder*. Hurrah!

TRUE STORIES: ELLIE

When July rolls around, the internet seems to consist of nothing but lists of things to do during the school holidays. I constantly feel like I should be doing elaborate scavenger hunts, baking rainbow cakes and making dreamcatchers out of foraged driftwood. In reality, of course, we while away most days watching TV and hanging out in Homebase.

I already have one son at school, but my youngest is still a toddler. Despite the fact that it's a while off, I feel wobbly even thinking about packing him off, too. But sometimes – on the days when it's too hot, and we're too tired and there have been three meltdowns by 10AM, and that's only counting mine – I do idly fantasise about what I'll do with all that free time. So here's a bucket list of things I plan to do once both my children are at school.

1. Have a Poo in Peace
I will enter the bathroom. I will close the door. I may or may not lock it. And I will enjoy the thrill of having a poo without being asked what I'm doing, or how long I will be, or where the pirate cutlass is, or whether we've got any Dairylea Dunkers, or how to put Wolverine's legs back on. It will feel more luxurious than a weekend at The Ritz.

2. Save Millions on the Weekly Shop
I look forward to leaving the supermarket with only the healthy, essential foods we need to live: like bread, eggs and Sauvignon Blanc. I won't have to bribe and argue my way around the shop, nor end up with a trolley full of half-eaten Cheestrings and packets of Bear Yoyos. Not to mention those weird yoghurt lollies that look like feet, which they absolutely love and which cost £17 each.

3. Have Lunch
As in a proper lunch, not a packet of crisps and some out-of-date hummus. I may even eat it in a restaurant. There will be wine.

4. Read a Book

An actual grown-up book. It will feature no Gruffalos, hungry caterpillars or pirate dinosaurs. No flaps to lift or songs to sing. No narratives based around the tediously implausible idea that a zoo would post a series of exotic and dangerous animals to a small child on request. I will read a novel, perhaps that new Harper Lee one, or that obscure Nabokov I never got round to. I definitely won't finish the *50 Shades of Grey* series or re-read *Twilight*.

5. Have a Cry

Because lovely though these things are, none of them are as good as spending time with my children. I know that when I come home from that first double drop-off, I'll close the front door and weep for the absence of my little ones. I'll cry for five years of love and laughs and companionship, and yes, the tantrums too. (Although I might not shed tears for the days when potty training went wrong.)

I will count the hours till I can collect them and ask my littlest about his first day. I won't mind when he won't tell me anything. I will hold him close and sniff his hair, and breathe in the strange new smell of school. I will kiss his tired, beautiful face and tell them I've got some of those weird feet lollies in the fridge, if they fancy it. Then we'll do it all again the next day, and I know it will get easier.

In the meantime, this is my summer holiday bucket list: to store up as many memories as possible. Not of elaborate crafts or exotic adventures, but of my children as they are now – the endless questions, the daft jokes, the feeling of the littlest's arms around my neck, the way the big one's hair curls over his ears when it rains. The most important item on my list is to remember my sons as best I can in all their funny, gorgeous glory.

Well, that, and to actually buy something from Homebase. I'm pretty sure the security guard is on the point of throwing us out.

FANTASY VS REALITY: STARTING SCHOOL

As with so many aspects of parenting, our preconceived ideas about what having a child at school means can be quite different from it's actually like. Here's a useful guide for parents gearing up for that first term.

Fantasy	Reality
Your child will be on time for school every day. You will be standing at the gates five minutes before they open, having a lovely calm chat with the other parents. You will be wearing a freshly pressed Breton top and mascara.	You will quickly realise success means getting out of the door without shouting, and with shoes on. You will arrive at the school gates with seconds to spare, huffing and puffing, still wearing your pyjamas, with Coco Pops in your hair.
Your child will be dressed in neatly ironed matching co-ordinates every day, including the relevant pair of days-of-the-week pants.	By half-term, you'll be congratulating yourself if your child is wearing a pair of trousers without a hole in, and has pants on at all.
You will be a valuable member of the school community, manning the tombola at the fête, preparing delicious trays of frangipane for bake sales and making bunting.	You will turn up for the bake sale two hours late, hungover and clutching a packet of Ginger Nuts.
You will maintain a well-stocked art cupboard, ready to lovingly handcraft a wide variety of costumes for the Nativity, Book Week, Multicultural Day, etc.	You will fail to provide a single costume that was not made the day before with the help of Amazon Prime and an old sheet.

You look forward to relaxing, sophisticated evenings with your new mum friends, discussing the novels you're currently reading over a bottle of wine.

Actually, mums' nights out are a highlight of having a child at school. But forget the book group and the Merlot. You'll have more fun drinking cocktails and going dancing, scabbing a fag off the DJ and passing it round while talking about who is fitter – the bloke who comes in for the football coaching or the hipster dad with the nice bottom. Good times!

SCUMMY MUMMY CONFESSION

"My son shouted 'ARSEHOLE' as an answer in the PTA quiz."

TRUE STORIES: HELEN

Nobody tells you that when your kid starts school, not only do you get to spend Monday to Friday with their new friends and their parents – but also the ENTIRE WEEKEND! Saturdays and Sundays become a never-ending round of birthday parties in dusty church halls, sauna-like sports venues and soul-sucking soft-play centres. And no matter where the party is, it will be so loud your brain will start to leak out of your ears.

I'm sure things were different when we were kids. Back in the eighties, we were happy with pass the parcel and food with enough colouring to dye all the flags for Pride.

I miss the parties I had in my twenties, too. In those days it was all about cheap wine and uncomfortably tight clothing. I liked to impress people with my unique dance routines, mainly showcased in kitchens. This would be followed by an entire day of recovery involving lots of bacon and Coca-Cola.

These days it's all bouncy castles, face painting, piñatas, gluten-free fairy cakes and men called Ian pretending they're qualified to do 'Jedi training' because they're wearing a brown dressing gown.

And the birthday party arms race ramps up as the school year goes on. Your kids are only too aware that Oliver had the REAL Chewbacca at his party, and how Imogen's mummy took the whole class to the Build-a-Bloody-Bear Workshop. Cue lots of conversations like this:

"Mummy, I want a My Little Pony Party. Can we get real ponies to come to the house?"

"No, darling. We live in a two-bedroom semi in Catford."

"That's so unfair. You are the worst mum EVER!"

"I love you too, sweetheart."

I must admit, there have been times when I've been sucked into the whole thing myself. I've spent hours on Pinterest, searching for the perfect *Frozen* cupcake toppers, and telling myself that of course I have a spare three hours to spend carving a watermelon into the shape of Anna's face.

But things never work out quite like I planned, and if there's one thing I've learned about birthday parties, it's this: they will break you. By 5.03PM you will be hunched on the sofa, a quivering mess, drinking warm fizz out of an Elsa cup and nibbling on a half-chewed Hula Hoop you just found in your cleavage.

I think it's important there's fizz, though, or at least something for the grown-ups to drink. I try not to judge people, but if I'm honest, I do choose mum friends based on whether they serve alcohol at their kids' parties. It's a deal-breaker. Being in a room full of five-year-olds screaming their way through a sugar rush is only fun if you're also five years old, and otherwise only bearable if you've got some cheap Prosecco to take the edge off.

At least you're safe in the knowledge that once the E-numbers have worn off, your kids will sleep for a full 12 hours. In the meantime, you can eat your fill of Party Rings and Wotsits, and relax. Just don't think about the parties they'll have when they're teenagers.

SCUMMY MUMMY CONFESSION

"Sometimes, when it's P.E. day, I just spray the dirty kit I find with deodoriser, then fold it neatly back into the kit bag."

WHAT TO WEAR FOR THE SCHOOL RUN

Mornings can be a stressful time. It's hard to feel positive about the day ahead when you're woken up by having the *Bob the Builder* theme tune screamed in your face. Then there's the routine to get through – serving breakfast, making packed lunches, brushing teeth and/or hair, all while shouting "SHOES ON" so many times the neighbours must think that's your child's name.

With all that going on, the last thing you need to worry about is what to wear. So here are some easy Scummy Mummy looks you can pull together to look stylish on the school run.

Sports Casual
Throw on a loose sweatshirt, leggings and trainers for a look that says: "I'm going for a run straight after drop-off, or perhaps to a Bikram yoga class." Or more likely: "I've been too tired to do any laundry for the last fortnight, and these are the only things I could find that were vaguely clean. I haven't actually done any yoga since 2009."

Strictly Mum Dancing
Can't be bothered to get out of your pyjamas? Just put an evening gown over the top. Everyone will be too dazzled by the glamour to notice the Primark check poking out from underneath.

The Parisian
You can't go wrong with a Breton top, jeans and plimsoles for a bit of classic French chic. Not that many French people buy their jeans at the supermarket, or wear Converse older than their children.

The Hip Dad
Fathers can be fashionable, too! Wearing a Ramones T-shirt tells everyone you are still cool, despite the fact you only listen to music you liked in your twenties and don't even know what Spotify is.

ACTUAL TOP TIP

Miss M, primary-school teacher

"When you're spending all day with someone's child, you have quite a bit in common! So as a teacher, I appreciate parents who try to develop some kind of relationship with me (although I draw the line at Facebook friend requests).

"It's good to have a realistic understanding of your child's abilities. However, there's no need to put them down to avoid being 'the parent who bangs on about how great their child is'.

"Never slag off the previous year's teacher. Understand the fact there are 30-odd other kids in the class who are just as important. Try multiplying the time they spend with yours by 30 and see what you end up with.

"Be warm and friendly, as this is often how teachers gauge your opinion of them. And be appreciative of what they do. I love those parents who come into the classroom or shoot me an email to say 'thank you' at the end of each term. Most of all, never start a sentence with: 'I'm not one of those parents, but...'"

WOW Cards

If you've got a child at school or nursery, you're probably familiar with WOW cards. Parents are supposed to fill them out and hand them in to celebrate their children's achievements, like counting to ten, playing nicely, etc. But what if we were more honest with our WOW cards…?

WOW!

Name: Megan   24/3

Megan did a shit the exact size and colour of a whole chorizo.

WOW!

Name: Hugo   Date: 9/6

Hugo counted all the Happy Meal toys in the car. He got to 20!

WOW!

Name: Charlie   Date: 20/6

Charlie has learned to turn on Netflix all by himself.

WOW!

Name: Matilda   Date: 28/10

Matilda told the health visitor
we had carrot sticks and
hummus for lunch. (We
actually had fish fingers
and Angel Delight.)

WOW!

Name: Rosie   Date: 16/8

All the children were asked to
perform a poem or song for the
end-of-year assembly. Rosie
sang the music from the Go
Compare ad. So proud.

WOW!

Name: Joe   Date: 7/12

Joe took less than 25 minutes
to put his shoes on.

SCUMMY SINGALONG!

Struggling to cope with the constant demands to bake cakes, sew bunting, and make Easter bonnets for the school fair? Here's a happy little ditty to sing under your breath when it all gets too much.

SCHOOL PTA
BY THE SPILLAGE PEOPLE
(to the tune of *YMCA*)

Hey mum, so your kid started school
I said, hey mum, there are all these new rules
I know you don't, want to look like a fool
But don't think you have to join in

Look out, here comes Lynne from 3P
She wants you to, be on the committee
For the spring fair, and the school spelling bee
But you're best off out of that shit

Just stay away from the school PTA
Just stay away from the school PTA
They will make you bake cakes
They will make you run stalls
You'll be climbing the playground walls

School PTA
Just stay away from the school PTA
You've got too much to do
With your precious spare time
Like watch telly and guzzle wine

Look mum, there's no need to be sad
I said, hey mum, don't feel guilty or bad
You should man up, and behave like a dad
And ignore those endless emails

Hey mum, let's just cancel the fair
Cos it's more than, any of us can bear
Let's be honest, none of the kids will care
If there's no bloody tombola

Just stay away from the school PTA
Just stay away from the school PTA
Look we're glad they exist
And we know they mean well
But school fêtes are a living hell

School PTA
Just stay away from the school PTA
Let's all go down the pub
Screw the raffle and quiz
Spend the kitty on chips and fizz
School PTA!

HELLO, PRE-MUM ME: ARE YOU STILL IN THERE?

There's a lot of pressure on mums these days. We're supposed to devote our whole beings to our children while simultaneously having a great career, running a tidy home and looking great in jeggings.

On top of that, we're expected to defy biology and the passing of time and 'bounce back' to our pre-baby selves. The truth is that once you've had a child, nothing ever bounces again – it just flaps, sways and jiggles.

And forget all these face creams promising to 'add 70 per cent more moisture and actively reduce the visible signs of ageing'. Top tip: you can achieve that by having a bath in the dark. And that way you get to have a wank and a cake.

But somewhere among the piles of washing and mountains of Mega Bloks, beyond the stained cardigan and the unbrushed hair, inside, *you're still you*. Except you're not you, of course – you're someone who's been fundamentally and permanently altered by the experience of having a child, and you'll never be able to watch *One Born Every Minute* without crying again. Or, for that matter, *Homes Under the Hammer*.

The trick is to look after yourself. This is often easier said than done, especially when our old friend Dr Guilt is whispering in your ear: "Why are you wasting all this time shaving your legs? You should be cleaning up the kitchen and teaching them phonics!"

SCUMMY MUMMY CONFESSION

"I let one off in Lidl and blamed the baby."

Try to remember, though, that if you're screwed, your children are screwed anyway. Part of being a good mum is trying to ensure you're physically and mentally well enough to be there for your kids. And this means different things for different people – for some it's meditation and exercise; for others it's watching old episodes of *Murder, She Wrote* while eating a whole Viennetta.

Having a child doesn't transform you into a different person overnight. Anyone who expects to cough out a baby and suddenly find they're some sort of cross between Mary Poppins and Gwyneth Paltrow is likely to be disappointed. Becoming a mum is about learning as you go along, working out who you are now, and adjusting to the fact it's not all about you any more. If you can do all that without losing yourself in the process, at least some of the time – you're winning.

SCUMMY MUMMY CONFESSION

"I pretend to go to the loo so I can lock the door and have some peace. I once did this five times in a two-hour period."

DO YOU HAVE AN ASS PROBLEM?

Are you an over-sharer? Are you the person at the party who misjudges the flow of the conversation and tells an embarrassing story that creates a fog of discomfort, silencing the room? If you have no filter between your thoughts and your mouth, then you, dear friend, suffer from the serious condition of Awkward Sharer Syndrome (ASS).

It's a gift, really. Being able to make others laugh with stories of humiliation and failure is such fun. But it's easy to forget that people don't always want to hear about the time you fanny-farted in a yoga class, especially when they just met you 90 seconds ago at a bus stop.

You'll find your ASS can flare up at any time. For example, Scummy Mummy Helen was once chatting to a teacher at school about the importance of making sure her son could get his P.E. kit on by himself. The teacher explained that trying to single-handedly get 30 four-year-olds dressed was proving a bit tricky.

Most people would smile and nod sympathetically at this, and that's what Helen did. But because of her ASS, she then added: "Oh God, you poor darling, what a FUCKING NIGHTMARE!" This was followed with a huge laugh that died away as she noticed all the other kids and parents staring at her, and the teacher looking horrified. Damn you, ASS.

No one who's got ASS deliberately creates a weird atmosphere, or wants to scar people forever. It's like a strange compulsion, one you just have to cope with, and even embrace. Celebrate the fact you live your life on the rollercoaster of shame – it may be bumpy, it may induce nausea, but it's never dull.

So if you feel like spicing up your life with a bit of ASS, here is our seven-step programme for over-sharing.

Step One:
Have a normal conversation with a human.

Step Two:
Enjoy the conversation. Maybe even make the person laugh.

Step Three:
Get too confident. Make a reference to something stupidly awkward, e.g. sex, bowel movements, or youthful drug taking. Other options include totally misjudging the other person's political bias, and excessive swearing.

Step Four:
Soak up the awkward silence as the other human stares at the ground in horror.

Step Five:
Laugh weirdly and blush. Exit.

Step Six:
Be wracked with shame. Lose sleep. Find yourself literally shuddering every time the incident comes to mind, which happens about 18 times a day.

Step Seven:
Repeat for the rest of your life, until you actually die of embarrassment.

BONUS POINT:
Put it in a book, so everyone knows about your ASS problem.

SCUMMY MUMMY
CONFESSION

"I entered a village craft competition in their name. They won."

TRUE STORIES: ELLIE

By the time my first son was 18 months old, things had settled down. He was sleeping through the night, I was back at work part-time, and I felt like I was finally getting a handle on this whole mum thing. Everything was ticking over nicely. So obviously, I decided now was a great time to embark on a prosperous career in stand-up comedy.

"You want to do WHAT?" said my husband, as if I hadn't just shown him an advert for a comedy course, but a flight plan for a solo crossing of the Atlantic in a biplane made of straws. (In retrospect, this would have been less challenging.)

I'd always secretly wondered if I could do comedy. My dad is a comedian, so I grew up around stand-up, but I was afraid to give it a try. The problem with shooting for your dream is that if you miss, there goes your dream. Isn't it better to have the hope you might be good at something than the knowledge you're rubbish at it? (I know, I should be a motivational speaker.)

But there's nothing like having a child to focus the mind, strengthen the resolve and act as a reminder that we are all just insignificant bags of mortal flesh inching closer to death with every second that passes. (Again, I should probably paste this over a photo of a sunset and stick it on Facebook.)

The idea of telling a joke to a roomful of people in a pub seemed like nothing compared to pushing a human out of my vagina. But more importantly, it didn't matter now if I failed. Losing the fantasy would be OK, because I was happy with my reality. No matter what happened, there was always my lovely baby to go home to.

So, with the help of my husband, who was very supportive once he'd finished cleaning up the tea he'd spat out, I did the comedy course, and then started doing regular open-mic gigs. I loved it.

And it turned out it didn't really matter whether I was any good or not – it was brilliant to have a reason to get out of the house, to do something that was just for me. Also it helped that this always involved going to a pub.

It wasn't always easy, though. There were plenty of nights when I'd much rather have stayed at home than trek across London to tell a funny story about my episiotomy to three Spanish exchange students, an old man, and a dog. It was a struggle to pretend I was totally cool with not going on till 10.30PM, knowing there was still the long journey home to get through, and then the inevitable dawn wake-up call from my son.

I was whinging about this one night to another comedian. "I wish I'd started doing this in my twenties," I said. "It would have been so much easier."

"But you wouldn't have been ready then," he said. "You didn't have the confidence, or the material. The life experiences you've had have made you the person you are today, and now is your time." Now HE should be a motivational speaker.

Doing comedy started out as a hobby, but it's ended up being so much more for me. I'm glad I had enough support to be able to carve out something for myself.

SCUMMY MUMMY CONFESSION

"The first card my son ever made me was:
'GET OVER YOUR
HANGOVER SOON.'"

THE SMUG MUM TRANSLATOR

Every now and then, you meet a mum who seems to have it all
sorted. She's confident in her parenting style, relaxed in her attitude
and unafraid to wear white jeans. What's more, she's kind enough
to explain how you're doing it all wrong – in the nicest possible
way. But that's not always the whole story. Here's our guide to what
Smug Mum says, and what she really means.

Smug Mum says	Smug Mum means
"I've had two natural childbirths. I breastfed both my babies till they were two."	"I can no longer sneeze with confidence. My boobs are as long as my arms. When I'm on all fours, I'm actually on all sixes."
"I didn't need any stitches. It's probably because of all that perineal massage we did."	"My vagina is only good for storage. Last weekend I went to a kid's birthday party, got a bit tipsy, and sat on a space hopper. It disappeared."
"We don't own a television."	"She watched four hours of *Dora the Explorer* YouTube videos on my iPhone last night."
"It's great that your parenting style is so easy-going and fun."	"You are failing at this and your kids will end up in prison."
"Well, you know, he wanted a superhero-themed thing, and it was no effort really. I guess I just enjoy being creative."	"I spent seven hours researching 'Spider-Man birthday party' on Pinterest. Last night I was up till 3AM, drawing webs on Mini Babybels with a Sharpie and crying."
"I love that my children are such free spirits who know how to express themselves."	"I know my kids are shits. I am sorry. Please help me."

SCUMMY MUMMY CONFESSION

"I once tried on my daughter's
Elsa dress and got stuck.
She was furious. I started
laughing, which made the dress
rip. In the end I had to cut
myself out of it."

SCUMMY MUMMY CONFESSION

"My three-year-old was
drawing a picture on the Tube
one day. 'What's that you're
drawing, darling?' I said.
'YOUR VAGINA,' he replied."

TRUE STORIES: HELEN

Non-parents can be so cruel, can't they? Specifically, me. Pre-kids, I remember promising myself that when I became a mother, I wouldn't be one of those women who 'let herself go'. (What a bloody awful phrase.) There was no way I would give up my skinny jeans, or stop cutting my hair asymmetrically, or waxing everything.

Back then, though, things were different. I studied history of art, worked in galleries, wore too much black and smoked fancy cigarettes. Basically, I thought I was in a wanky French film. What a dork I was... But that dork got to read books, learn languages, visit confusing exhibitions, pierce things, flirt badly, wear dangly earrings and uncomfortable underwear and daydream.

Then I became a mum, and my watchwords switched from 'cool and interesting' to 'sensible and achievable'. And why not? I was exhausted and my boobs were dripping with milk. I happily swapped those jeans for practical chinos. I realised it doesn't matter what length your hair is when you're tying it back anyway. And I decided a bit of hair in other places never hurt anyone. In short, I became the polar opposite of the pre-mum me.

It's not that I haven't tried – I have dabbled in rediscovering myself (no, that isn't a euphemism for wanking). But I find myself spending those odd afternoons off wandering round the shops in a daze, not knowing where to go or what I should be wearing and end up buying a pair of orthopaedic shoes. Or I stay at home, determined to put my feet up and relax, just as soon as I've put a wash on, defrosted some mince and cleared out the spare room.

Don't get me wrong – I am so grateful to have had the opportunity to be at home with my kids and I love it, most of the time. But a few years down the line, I have started to miss the part of me that existed before I became the bum-wiping, tantrum-soothing ninja I am today.

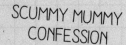

SCUMMY MUMMY CONFESSION

"While I was getting a manicure, the lady told me I had chocolate under my nails. I hadn't eaten chocolate that day."

Maybe it's because I'm finally getting some sleep, or because I'm approaching 40, but I feel like I'm emerging from the mum fog. I want more than pizza crusts for dinner; I want reading material that's more intellectually stimulating than the Toys-R-Us catalogue. I know, I'm so needy.

Now both my kids are at school, I have some time to myself at last. It's a bit scary, to be honest. What do I do? Who the hell am I these days, anyway?

I don't have any more excuses. I am going to get a bit of the pre-mum me back. My plan is to set myself achievable weekly challenges. Nothing too extreme – I won't be spending mornings at the Tate Modern before heading home to practise the cello. But I am going to try to do things that are nothing to do with the kids, and get back into the practice of putting me first. Instead of play dates, I will have grown-up dates with friends. We will talk about politics, fashion, art and music, and NOT ABOUT FUCKING HOUSE PRICES.

So that's where you'll find me – in Soho, having intelligent conversations over proper coffee, with not a babyccino in sight. You will, I promise. Just as soon as I've put a wash on.

ACTUAL TOP TIP

Zoë de Pass, fashion blogger, mum of two, and creator of DRESSLIKEAMUM.com

"When you become a mum, you obviously have more responsibilities. It's not about you any more. But it's easy to forget that you're still you.

"One of the things that helped me to keep hold of my identity was my clothes. Regardless of how tired I was, if I was wearing an outfit I felt good in, I had a slightly better day.

"The trick to "dressing like a mum" is simple – it's how you have always dressed. The mum thing is irrelevant. You should wear exactly what you want, and whatever makes you happy.

"There are a few practical tips that can help. Wearing vests is a good idea if you're breastfeeding – the top goes up, the vest comes down, the bra unclips, and the baby clips on. Dungarees and jumpsuits are great for this too, as well as hiding mumbums and mumtums.

"Don't save too many clothes for best. You'll be attending fewer posh parties and nice dinners, so you might as well get use out of them. Shop your wardrobe and dress things down.

"The most important thing about dressing like a mum is that you're happy and confident. If you feel like this you'll have a better day, no matter what you're wearing."

SCUMMY MUMMY CONFESSION

"I sneaked wine into a concert in my child's Tommee Tippee."

I NEED A VINO
(to the tune of *I Need a Hero*)

Every day I wake at dawn
When kids jump on my head
It takes me all damn morning
Just to get them dressed and fed
All day long I wonder
Why did I decide to breed?
By 5PM I'm mad and I'm sad
And I know just what I need

CHORUS
I need a vino
I'm crying out for a vino almost every night
Don't care if it's cheap
Don't care if it's nice
Don't care if it's red or it's white
I need a vino
I'm crying out for a vino almost every night
It's gotta be soon
And it's gotta be strong
And it's gotta be served in a pint
Served in a pint

Sometimes when the kids are out
I dream I'll change the locks
Lie down on the kitchen floor
And drink wine from a box
I don't need no handbooks
On how to be a mum
I just need a glass of wine
Or maybe a magnum

REPEAT CHORUS UNTIL DRUNK

MEET THE
ACTUAL
EXPERTS

We would like to thank all our wonderful experts for their contributions to this book. Many of them have also been guests on the *Scummy Mummies* podcast. Here's how to find out more about them.

Alison Sakai
Alison is the finance director at Firebox.com. She lives in South London with five-year-old Milly, who recently announced she would like to be a circus strongwoman when she grows up.
Twitter: @alisonsakai
Instagram: @alisonsakai

Carolyn Robertson
Mother-of-two Carolyn is the author of *Two Dads* and *Two Mums and a Menagerie*. She also writes the Sparkly Poo blog about her experiences as an adoptive mum.
Website: sparklypoo.com
Twitter: @CarolynAdopt

Clemmie Hooper
Clemmie is a midwife and mother of four. She is the author of the successful blog Gas and Air, where she shares her knowledge and wisdom on all things pregnancy, birth and mothering. Her first book, *How to Grow a Baby and Push It Out*, is available now.
Website: gasandairblog.com
Twitter: @midwifeyhooper
Instagram: @mother_of_daughters

George McEncroe
Writer, teacher, broadcaster and comedian George is a single mum to four teenagers. She is also the founder of women's-only ride-share Shebah and Mum's Taxi.
Twitter: @georgemcencroe

Helen McGinn

Having spent almost a decade as a supermarket winé buyer, Helen went on to write the award-winning blog and best-selling book *The Knackered Mother's Wine Club*. Her desert-island wine would be a bottle of 1988 vintage Champagne. Her desert-island dish would not be leftover fish fingers.

Website: knackeredmotherswineclub.com
Twitter: @knackeredmutha
Instagram: @knackeredmother

Inga Lyon

With a decade of nannying experience, Inga knows everything from a whinge-free way to apply suncream to how to make a three-year-old nap on your lap in a busy Pizza Express. This book would not have been written without her.

Jessie McCulloch

A health visitor, children's nurse and mum. Jessie uses her own experiences of being a less-than-perfect parent and medical professional to teach nurses in child health.

Jo Travers

Otherwise known as The London Nutritionist, Jo is a state-registered dietitian with a First Class BSc (Hons) in Human Nutrition & Dietetics. She has been in private practice for five years, and has consulted for the BBC and Channel 4, amongst others.

Website: thelondonnutritionist.co.uk

Sarah Lorentzen

Also known as The Fanny Physio, Sarah Lorentzen is a physiotherapist who has specialised for many years in all things vajingo, foo-foo and fanoir. Ironically she recently moved Down Under, but still runs her London-based pregnancy fitness business, Maternally Fit, from afar.

Website: maternallyfit.co.uk

Shannon-Kate Archer

Shannon-Kate Archer has worked as an employment lawyer in both Australia and the UK. She now lives in Melbourne with her husband and two children, where she is working to change the gender pay gap.

Steve Hill

Writer, raconteur, bell-end. Steve spent years touring the world in luxury in the name of journalism. He now sits in playgrounds staring into middle space, wondering how he became a stay-at-home dad.

Twitter: @HillyTheFish

Tracey Davies

As a veteran travel writer, Tracey regularly contributes to national newspapers, glossy magazines and colouring books. She lives in Brighton with her husband, son and identical twin girls.

Website: traceydavies.co.uk
Twitter: @dollysday
Instagram: @therealdollysday

Zoë de Pass

Based in London, Zoë is a fashion, beauty and kidswear blogger. She is the founder of Dress Like a Mum, and works to change the reputation of mum dressing. A mother of two, she enjoys getting out and about with (and without) the kids.

Website: dresslikeamum.com
Twitter: @ZdP
Instagram: @dresslikeamum

Rod and Rod

These Right-On Dads met at a La Leche seminar titled 'Breastfeeding for Men'. (They didn't even have kids then, but they wanted to be really prepared.) Together they run YouTube channel Greenwich Mentime – 'For men who live in Greenwich'. They have four children between them – Cassius and Lazarus, and Merlin and Mooncup.

Twitter: @rightondads
Instagram: @rightondads

Foofy St. Clair

Blogger and mumprepreneur Foofy lives in Fulham with her many dogs and some children. Her hobbies include making lovely cakes, buying things and hashtags.

Twitter: @foofystclair
Instagram: @foofystclair
Website: cupcakesandpupcakesblog.wordpress.com

Judith Krank

Born in Yorkeys Knob, Queensland, Judith Krank is known throughout Australia and around the world for her relaxed approach to parenting. Her lifetime achievements include giving birth while floating on a lilo above the Great Barrier Reef, and being Craig McLachlan's doula.

Twitter: @JudithKrank
Instagram: @JudithKrank

Margot Chesney-Hooter

Margot spent much of her life running a farm in Kenya alongside her husband, Jonty. After returning to the UK he left her for his secretary, but the day before the divorce was due to be finalised, he was struck by lightning while climbing a tree. Margot turfed his fiancée out of the house and drove all the classic cars into the lake. She has also written some parenting books.

Twitter: @margotchesneyh
Instagram: @margotchesneyhooter

THANK YOU

During the writing of this book we got through 80 bottles of wine, 1,700 cups of tea, one case of tonsilitis, several cases of nits, an emergency appendectomy, two trips to Legoland, six podcast recordings, seven children's birthday parties, a car crash and 68 plates of chips.

We would like to thank The Montage, The Signal and the Perry Vale in Forest Hill for letting us sit around with our laptops for hours and only sometimes trying to up-sell us Prosecco.

Thank you to our husbands, Will and Pete, for giving us the time and space to write this book by doing so much childcare. Or as we like to call it, 'parenting'. Love you.

Thank you to Jane Garvey for featuring us on *Woman's Hour*, which is how our lovely agent, Victoria Marshallsay, first heard of us. We are very grateful to Victoria, and to Céline at Quadrille, for making this book happen.

Thank you to all the people who have looked after our children while we dick about and type out boob jokes. Especially Ellie's mum, Ray, whose support for the Scummy Mummies has included not only loads of childcare but making fake baked beans and papier-mâché chorizo.

And to the rest of our parents – Jim, Tim and Lee – thank you for all the love and effort you put into raising us. We now know how much hard work it is, and we're sorry.

Thank you to everyone who's ever listened to our podcast, come to one of our shows and shared a Scummy Mummy Confession. We are so grateful for the emails and tweets we receive – they give us the motivation to keep going. Here's to you, fellow Scummies.

Most of all, thank you to our children. We love you very much.